HARTZELL SPENCE

No one is better equipped to write a definitive book on religions than Hartzell Spence, author of the best-selling novel, *One Foot in Heaven*. This classic, based upon his father's life in the ministry, was made into a motion picture which has been shown and re-run all over the world.

His other books include *Get Thee Behind Me, Vain Shadow, Happily Ever After, Bride of the Conqueror* and *The Big Top*.

During World War II Mr. Spence was executive editor of *Yank, the Army Weekly,* then special assistant to the commanding general, 20th Air Force.

Recently, he has been engaged in freelance writing—his principal assignment during the past two years being the preparation of LOOK Magazine's series of articles on great religions. These articles are incorporated in this book.

THE STORY OF
AMERICA'S RELIGIONS

THE
STORY OF
AMERICA'S
RELIGIONS

BY HARTZELL SPENCE

Published
In co-operation with the Editors
of LOOK Magazine

HOLT, RINEHART AND WINSTON • NEW YORK

Published simultaneously in Canada by
HOLT, RINEHART AND WINSTON OF CANADA, LIMITED.

FIRST EDITION

Acknowledgments

The author wishes to express his appreciation to Cowles Magazines, Inc. for permission to reprint these articles which originally appeared in LOOK, and to thank specifically the following editors and photographers: William B. Arthur, Frank Bauman, Cal Bernstein, Laura Bergquist, Chandler Brossard, Patricia Carbine, Paul Fusco, James Hansen, Daniel D. Mich, Phillip Harrington, Allen Hurlburt, Douglas Jones, Betty Leavitt, Bob Lerner, Robert Meskill, Thomas B. Morgan, Ira Mothner, Jack Star, Earl Theisen, John Vachon, Peter Van Slingerland, Bob Vose, Gereon Zimmermann and David Zingg.

The photograph which appears on the cover has been provided through the courtesy of the Abby Aldrich Rockefeller Folk Art Collection.

Library of Congress Catalog Card Number 60-12319
35126
Printed in the United States of America

Contents

v

42269

Foreword

To a remarkable degree, the United States is the product of religious impacts. In a very real sense, our social patterns are the result of religious beliefs and customs translated into democratic action. The social face of America would be profoundly different except for these emphases. The Congregational Way imposed Puritanism on New England, and ever since then puritannical restraints have interacted upon American life. The Church of England tradition entrenched a country-gentleman culture on the pre-Civil War South, particularly in Virginia and South Carolina. Roman Catholic foundations in Louisiana and New Mexico, and Father Serra's missions in California, saturated wide areas in non-Reformation attitudes. Catholic immigration vitally influenced city politics and the national labor movement. The Baptists shaped the deep South. In more limited locales, the upper Midwest is dominated by the traditions of Lutheranism, and great sections of Utah and Idaho are culturally Mormon. The Methodists rode across the Alleghanies with the pioneers, and founded enclaves which still react upon local ordinances, the election of public officials, and the American passion for social service.

It is often argued that religion per se did not produce these results, but that they were caused by immigrant groups which just happened, among other things, to share certain religious views. The reverse is more often true, as the studies in this book prove. Many events transpired because, at certain times and at certain places, religion motivated attitudes and events which have had permanent effects on American life. Seventy million Americans sometimes act as they do, and sometimes vote as they do, because they are Baptists, Methodists, Roman Catholics, Mormons, Christian

Scientists, Presbyterians, Seventh-day Adventists or Jews. Their thought processes react to certain religiously-ingrained stimuli, whether consciously or not. These reactions may even be violent. The Puritans hanged Quakers in Boston. Protestants mobbed Catholics in Quaker Philadelphia. Catholics fought pitched battles against Anglicans and Lutherans in Maryland. Protestants massacred Mormons in Missouri and Illinois. Jews have been tormented by discrimination. All these actions, as Everett Clinchy points out, have been taken "in the name of God."

On the shining face of the coin are many positive accomplishments. The Protestant passion for human equality motivated the crusade for the political and social emancipation of American womanhood. Christ's mercy spanned the land with Roman Catholic, Lutheran and Methodist hospitals. Until 1932, concern for human welfare was almost completely in the hands of religious bodies. The Hebraic compulsion for philanthropy and the arts founded scores of charitable and cultural centers. Many other examples are detailed in the studies that follow. All were launched and now are supported by persons and groups as witnesses to their faith.

The chief religions of America—Protestant, Roman Catholic, Jewish and Eastern Orthodox—are in essence dynamic. They must reach out, make impact, convert followers, influence events and uphold staunchly the great tenets of their faith. These activities have been protected and mothered by the Constitution of the United States. Here the call of conscience, the freedom of thought, speech and movement essential to religious life, have been nurtured to a phenomenal degree. No other political structure in world history has been so tolerant that it has incubated and legally protected 255 organized religious groups within its borders, giving equal opportunity to all and preference to none.

To this eclectic collection of churches, denominations and sects must also be added nearly four in ten Americans who, equally protected by government, openly avow no religion at all without fear of reprisal. The Constitution guarantees not only religious freedom as an inalienable right, but irreligious freedom as well. Until the mid-twentieth century, a majority of all Americans were unchurched, and thirty-nine per cent still are. This, too, is a phenomenon that has influenced the American culture. The unbeliever may speak up, creating thrust and counterthrust against religion. Freedom of heresy compels religious groups, particularly the Christians, to be even more zealous in their witness, and causes them to reiterate their message with fervor to each succeeding generation.

No attempt has been made in the following study of fourteen religious emphases to survey the entire field of religions in America. Such would be impossible within the limitations of a single magazine series. The intent of the author and the editors of *Look* magazine was to select those denominations and churches which have made great sociological impacts upon the American scene. Religious freedom is dear to every American, whether he is religious or not. If he is not, he cherishes his right to disbelief. How true, then, the editors asked, is the often-cited assertion that the United States is a Christian nation? What precisely have Christianity in its many forms, and Judaism the harbinger of Christianity, contributed to the so-called American way of life?

The pursuit of these questions required three years of study, 205,577 miles of travel in the United States by myself and *Look* researchers and photographers, conversations in snow-isolated monasteries, missionary outposts, slums and saloons, penthouses and parsonages, in seminars and forums, on farms and in villages, with several thousand persons. All of them, in some way or other, were living their faith, not merely with lip service and small coins, but with great dedication and sacrifice. I went to them on the thesis that the living history of any religion is the actions of the people who worship within it, rather than the decisions of the theologians. The library research involved the reading of more than 2,000 church histories, 3,600 manuscripts, 8,000 newspapers, magazines, journals, diaries, letters and other source materials, and the help of scholars who translated for me from Hebrew, Greek, German, Russian, Romanian and Arabic sources.

Twelve *Look* photographers covered 26 states and took more than 30,000 photographs from which 153 were selected to illustrate the series. In addition, the editors commissioned 14 oil paintings by Aaron Bohrod, a noted American artist. His work in the fine arts has received wide acclaim, and he is represented in the collections of most major American museums, including the Metropolitan Museum of Art, the Walker Art Center of Minneapolis, the Art Institute of Chicago, the Museum of Fine Arts in Boston, the Detroit Institute of Arts.

Each painting in the series depicts in *trompe l'oeil* style the major historic artifacts of the American development of one of the religions. The location and selection of these artifacts was in itself a major research project.

Significant accolades resulted from the series. These included the 1959 and 1960 National Brotherhood Awards of the National Conference of Christians and Jews, the Freedoms Foundation's 1959 and 1960 Distinguished Service Awards, the National Religious Publicity Council's magazine award for 1959, and the Periodical Distributors of America Association's Maggie Award for family service in 1959.

Two important areas of American religious life were not penetrated in this study. The first is the growing ecumenical movement, the gradual coming together of Protestant Christian bodies by merger or joint action. This is evidenced by the flourishing National Council of the Churches of Christ in America, and by the World Council of Churches. A collateral movement, in the author's opinion significant, is the growing number of local communions which have thrown down their competitiveness, merged in a local area for more effective service, and today carry on as Christian communities without organizational allegiance. This ecumenical spirit, of moving forward in the name of Christ rather than under a denominational banner, is gaining in momentum and stature.

The other unpenetrated area is the contribution made to American religious life and social culture by the myriad smaller groups, chiefly Protestant, which minister to millions

whom the big denominations neglect or reject. There is a
multitude of them: slum churches in vacant stores in which
dedicated workers preach Christ to people who would never
enter the Gothic edifices of the comfortable middle class;
little town churches which preach fundamentalism with
emotional fervor; the revival preachers on street corners and
under rural tents; the radio and television evangelists whose
sermons fill the air every Sunday morning. Some of these
voices are well organized and thriving, as the Churches of
God and the Churches of Christ; others are one-man or
husband-wife team efforts by individuals of remarkable zeal.
All serve Christ in their own way.

The question most often asked me during this project
was whether, according to my present studies, I thought
there was any likelihood of Christianity's reuniting into one
great movement, freed of the denominationalism and the
variety of emphases which now exist. I must confess that
I found no visible evidence of such a possibility in the
foreseeable future.

The history of religions in America tends to support a
thesis that as rapidly as groups merge, new divisions develop.
A case in point—and it is merely one of many—is the recent
merger of the Congregational-Christian Churches with the
Evangelical and Reformed Church. This project moves
forward; but at least two hundred congregations will not
join it. What, then, will they do? They will retain their
congregationalism, of course, and so there will be one more,
instead of one less, group.

But is this unfortunate? The vogue these days is for
church leaders to think in terms of unity. The Universalists
and Unitarians merged in 1959, and at least a half dozen
other important corporate unions are under study. There
have been many such consolidations in the past twenty years.
Pope John XXIII issued a call for ecumenical explorations
in one of the first pronouncements of his reign. The Disciples
of Christ, and the Presbyterians, work ceaselessly for Christian unification, as do the Eastern Orthodox churchmen.
However, religion is an intensely personal experience, perhaps the deepest of all human responses. It is only human

for some worshipers to find inspiration and comfort in one emphasis and some in another. The dogmatism of Lutheranism is unacceptable to the individualistic type of mind which is comfortable in Methodism. The intellectual to whom Unitarianism has great appeal would be lost in a revival tent.

Perhaps the virility which now characterizes American religious life would wither in a united church. The individual tends to lose his identity in a monolithic religious structure. Either he becomes mystically submerged in the whole, or he pays it only lip service. Or as a desperate measure, he separates from it into the depths of his own heart, there to work out a lonely rationalization of his unique position. Perhaps the very essence of American Christianity—freedom of religion—would cease to have significant meaning in a united church.

Today, in America, no one has far to go to find religious expression. As long as there are religious edifices on almost every street, in one of which you and I, and the scholar, the ignorant, the literalist, the liberal, the rich, the poor, may worship and witness in his own sincerity, there will be inspiration and solace for everyone who yearns for a religious experience. That, in itself, makes every organized religious accent important.

H. S.

1

The Methodists

IF ALL THE METHODISTS in the United States were to march down New York's Fifth Avenue ten abreast and in ranks ten yards apart, the parade would stretch for 524 miles and take ten days and nights to pass a reviewing stand. Marching would be 18 United States senators, 85 congressmen, 14 state governors, 9,000 college professors, 2,710,000 Negroes, plus a fair quota of America's wealthiest citizens and some 10,000 American Indians. Out front, without doubt, would be 1,842,000 members of one of the strongest women's clubs in the world, the Woman's Society of Christian Service.

What's more, if Methodists were convinced that by so marching they could advance the cause of Christ anywhere in the world, they would march—every one of them. For they are the great doers of United States Protestantism, pioneers in the crusades for such social ideals as world peace, racial equality, the rights of labor and Christian unity. They sparked the movements for national prohibition and for women's suffrage, against the sweatshop and child labor. Before World War II had even ended, through ninety mass meetings held in a Crusade for a New World Order, they helped immeasurably to create a climate of American public opinion favorable to the United Nations.

The first religious publishing house on the continent was Methodist, and it is still the largest in United States Protestantism, with a brisk $22,500,000 annual business. Methodists have built 93 American colleges, nine universities, ten graduate schools of theology, 73 hospitals. They are the greatest Christian missionaries outside the Roman Catholic Church in the world today.

Methodism arrived in the United States almost 150 years after such denominations as the Congregationalists, but soon outstripped them all in numbers. The Methodist Church is still the largest single Protestant body in America, with a membership of 10,729,936.

It is a church of great flexibility, more devoted to action than aesthetics, preaching a simple, democratic gospel and little torn by doctrinal disputes. Thus in the twenty-three branches of Methodism there has been ample room for such diverse personalities as Kansas saloon buster Carry Nation; for the controversial Bishop James Cannon, Jr., who built the Virginia Anti-Saloon League to such power that it dominated state and, finally, national politics; for feminist and educator Frances E. Willard and for today's vocal left-winger, the Reverend Jack McMichael.

Methodism has more Negro than white members in New York City at a time when many Methodist laymen in the South are impassioned segregationists. It supports more colleges than any other Protestant denomination, though until 1800 not a single American Methodist preacher was a college graduate. Study and learning, it was felt, interfered with the basic job of soul-saving.

Today, its ministers range from the scholarly Dr. Lynn

Harold Hough, former dean of Drew Theological Seminary and author of forty books, to Ozark Mountain faith healers. A Methodist church may be the stylish, erudite Park Avenue congregation of the Reverend Dr. Ralph Sockman, whose preaching of the social gospel is well known to radio audiences, or an uninhibited fellowship whose members shout "Hallelujah" and "Amen" with true old-style emotionalism.

The church finds nothing strange or contradictory in this wide latitude in belief and approach. John Wesley, Methodism's English founder, who remained a priest in the Church of England until the day he died, set the pattern two hundred years ago with these words: "Methodists alone do not insist on your holding this or that opinion, but they think and let think."

"If your heart is with my heart, give me your hand," Wesley said. Indeed, the first Methodists, in both England and America, were groups of pious people *within* the Church of England, formed into societies for the promotion of holiness. Wesley was proud that no doctrinal tests were ever laid down for membership.

The word "Methodist" was originally a sarcastic barb aimed by fellow students of Oxford University at the manner in which Wesley and his friends pursued a strict regime of living from dawn to bedtime, their every action methodically planned to make them more godly. They were called, variously, Bible Bigots, Bible Moths, Methodists—and the last name stuck.

To join the Methodist Church today, you need only avow a belief in God, and in Jesus Christ as God's son

and every man's personal Saviour. From there, theologically, you are on your own. But Methodists have
personal responsibilities which affect their every action,
laid down in an 890-page Discipline, or constitution,
which is reviewed and revised every four years in General
Conference. Early Disciplines forbade dancing, card
playing, the use of tobacco and horse racing. (Until the
1888 Discipline, Methodists were adjured to dress so
simply that even a bit of lace on a petticoat or the wearing
of a gold ornament was deemed sinful.)

Above all, Methodists proclaim that all men are
equal in the sight of God and capable of being saved.
Quite naturally, then, does the church turn to missionary
work and social crusading.

President Theodore Roosevelt aptly summed up the
Methodist spirit in a speech at American University.
Methodism's "essential democracy," he said, "its fiery
and restless energy of spirit and the wide play it gave to
individual initiative, all tended to make it peculiarly congenial to a hardy and virile folk, democratic to the core,
prizing individual independence above all earthly possessions and engaged in the rough and stern work of
conquering a continent."

Historians agree that the pioneer Methodist preachers,
the remarkable breed of men known as circuit riders, were
greatly responsible for bringing order to the chaotic
frontier. As America swept West, Methodist parsons
moved right with the pioneers. It has been said that the
first human sound in the American wilderness was the
ring of the frontiersman's ax; the second was the "hello"
of the circuit rider. Tobias Gibson, assigned to the South-

west in 1798, rode horseback five hundred miles from central Tennessee to the Mississippi River, then swapped his mount for a canoe and paddled downstream to reach new settlements springing up in that region. He didn't report to his bishop for four years.

Rider William W. Van Orsdell, who built one hundred churches, fifty parsonages, six hospitals and two colleges in Montana and Idaho, one day found himself in a stagecoach holdup. He said to the bandit who sought his purse, "You wouldn't rob an old Methodist preacher, would you?" To which the robber replied, "Of course not, I'm a Methodist myself."

Peter Cartwright, whose bailiwick was Illinois, vowed he would visit every cabin in the territory and meet every immigrant on arrival. He preached 18,000 sermons, baptized 15,000 children, recruited 12,000 new members. In 1860, he wrote: "I have traveled its [Illinois'] prairies, slept with only the canopy of Heaven for cover. I have followed the trail of the Indians, fought desperadoes, swum rivers, threaded the pathless forests, in order that I might carry the tidings of the blessed Gospel to the loneliest cabin."

So appalling were the dangers faced by these early "men on horseback," called the "most interesting, self-sacrificing breed of men known to American history," that nearly half died before they were thirty. Of all the riders, the most intrepid by far was Francis Asbury, America's first Methodist bishop, sent from England by John Wesley himself as a missionary in 1771. Bedeviled all his life by boils and ulcers, Asbury traveled through heat and blizzard, logging 270,000 miles of ministry to the wilderness. His only address was "America."

Asbury rose at 4 A.M. daily and preached his first sermon an hour later. While in the saddle, he taught himself Latin, Greek and Hebrew. In 1816, at seventy, almost blind and hobbling on crutches from rheumatism, he was hoisted to his saddle for one last preaching mission in the Carolinas and Virginia. He fell from his horse and died at Spotsylvania, Virginia.

The riders preached to anyone who would listen, anywhere—in homes, barns, schools, courthouses and, in the West, even in saloons and bawdy-houses. James B. Finley, under fire in 1811 for holding services in an Ohio dance hall, said, "The gospel is to be preached to every creature, and I will go to any place this side of hell." He and his brethren opened their Bibles on packet boats and river rafts, on covered wagons and hillsides, in gristmills and warehouses.

Their welcome was not always warm. Rowdies, condemned for Sabbath breaking and indulging in the demon rum, often raided the meetings. Cartwright, who liked a good brawl, became famous for his technique of seizing two hecklers and cracking their skulls together. Philip Gatch, tarred and feathered by a mob near Bladensburg, Maryland, went to his appointed meeting, bleeding and tarred, and preached a two-hour sermon on forgiveness.

Because frontier life was hard and lonely, the arrival of the circuit rider drew a sociable gathering from 50 miles around. Preachers were also salesmen for the Methodist Book Concern and sold its books, magazines and "penny edifiers" on their rounds. They were also great exhorters, inspiring listeners to frenzies of shouting and singing, an emotional outlet for frontiersmen and their women enduring the rigors of a primitive life. Lorenzo Dow, founder of the Primitive Methodist Church, was disgruntled once by the tepid response of a South Carolina congregation during outdoor meetings. Covertly, he posted a boy in a treetop with a horn. At the climax of his sermon, which dealt with Judgment Day, he shouted, "Suppose you heard Gabriel's horn—would you be ready?" At this cue, there was a blast from the tree top. Many parishioners swooned, and 120 repented their sins. When the ruse was discovered, Dow proclaimed, "If a boy with a tin horn can frighten you out of your wits, what will you do when you hear the Archangel?"

The free-wheeling emotionalism of these early Methodists has enriched our common speech with several phrases—like "Amen Corner." Early frontier Methodism was organized into classes of twelve persons who met in a private home once a week to review their sins, pay their tithes and receive spiritual encouragement from their local lay leader, known as the "exhorter." When the circuit rider came to town, perhaps once a month, the exhorters sat together to the right of the pulpit and acted as a cheering section. They underscored the sermon with shouts of "Amen," "Hallelujah," "Praise the Lord," to warm up both preacher and congregation. Their reserved pew became known as the "Amen Corner."

The "anxious seat" is equivalent to the Army expression "sweating it out." No early Methodist preacher ever ended a sermon without calling upon sinners to come forward, confess their faults and join the faithful. Listeners who were inspired to repent would walk to a specially reserved front row. There they were immediately encircled by exhorters and friends who worked on them with all the zeal of a college fraternity team rushing a freshman. This front row, the "anxious seat"—where sinners waited for the Spirit to move them—was a fixture at Methodist revivals and the great camp meetings which swept the frontier at the beginning of the nineteenth century. After 150 years, it still survives among the Free Methodists, the Primitive Methodists and some Negro church bodies.

The democracy of Methodism was peculiarly suited to the frontier. Its promise of golden streets in a sweet by-and-by also held special appeal for a pioneer, who was likely to win little but hardship in this life. Until 1872, the Discipline made membership for a wealthy man almost impossible, by holding that accumulations of wealth were sinful. Meetinghouses were primitive and unadorned by steeples, bells or organs. A description of Methodist church furniture in Iowa in 1843 has been left by one Hiram Price, who wrote a friend back East: "The seats were free—free from upholstery, free from paint, free from backs. . . . The best were made of slabs from the sawmill, with flat side up. . . . They were the poorest kind of seats in which to take a nap during the sermon."

But such rigors only strengthened the faith of Methodists, who by 1860 numbered one American out of nineteen, making them the nation's largest and most evenly distributed church. Abraham Lincoln took notice of them from the White House in 1864. "It may fairly be said," he wrote, "that the Methodist Episcopal Church, not less devoted than the best, is by its greater numbers the most important of all. It is no fault in others that the Methodist Church sends more soldiers to the field, more nurses to the hospitals and more prayers to heaven than any. God bless the Methodist Church!"

A distinguishing quality of Methodists even today is their singing, which at a great church convocation is an experience no hearer ever forgets. Methodism, it has been said, literally sang itself into the hearts of the people. The roots of the tradition go back to Charles Wesley, brother of founder John Wesley, who wrote the words to 6,500 hymns.

Until the Methodists, there was little hymn singing in church as we know it now. Music was limited largely to chants and Te Deums. Charles Wesley wrote hymns for every conceivable occasion: for rising and retiring, for washing dishes and laundry, for hewing wood and plowing. His genius as a hymn writer lay in the intensely personal quality of his words, which bristle with personal pronouns. "Oh, for a thousand tongues to sing *my* great Redeemer's praise," "Jesus, lover of *my* soul"—these are the paeans of Methodism.

Pianos and organs were deemed unnecessary frills by the Methodists until long after the Civil War, but this was no deterrent to their singing. An exhorter or minister need only announce the first stanza of a hymn and add, "We will sing this to the tune of 'Miles Lane'." Someone with an accurate musical ear struck the first note, and the congregation took off with one voice. For those unfamiliar with the words, the minister shouted out each line just ahead of the singers.

This practice occasionally caused confusion. An aged circuit rider at Lake Mills, Iowa, in the 1870's entered his pulpit one morning, fumbled in vain for his spectacles and commented, "My eyes are dim, I cannot see." Immediately the congregation, cued by this line, began singing it. The surprised cleric, trying to make amends, shouted, "I did not mean that you should sing, but only that my eyes are dim." This line fitted the tune so everybody kept on going. The preacher gave up, entered into the spirit of the event and concluded, "This is no hymn to sing at all. I think the devil's got you all."

The men who preached the gospel were earthy, realistic men for the most part, plain and simple in their tastes, and willing to accept whatever hospitality the humblest settler's cabin afforded.

Peter Cartwright, returning to Springfield, Illinois, from a month of riding on the circuit, greeted street loafers with the question, "What's new?" One young man said innocently, "I suppose you came home for the funeral." Cartwright asked who had died. "Why," said the wag, "while you were away, the devil died." Cartwright smiled, reached for his purse and pulled out a penny. The jokester asked, "What's that for?" The circuit rider replied, "It's for you. My religion teaches me to be charitable to orphans."

During Cartwright's campaign for election to Congress, his opponent was a country lawyer named Abe Lincoln, who heckled him loudly during a campaign rally. Cartwright asked, "If you are not going to repent and go to heaven, where are you going?" "To Congress, Brother Cartwright, to Congress," said Lincoln and did so.

Methodism arose in England in 1739 as a protest against nearly every aspect of English life. It was the era of low private and public morals, brilliantly satirized by the eighteenth-century artist William Hogarth. Men and women worked in mines and factories in conditions of indescribable cruelty. Drunkenness was their most common escape (hence Methodism's early concern with temperance).

By 1769, when the crusading John Wesley first sent two official missionaries to America, robust Methodist societies were already flourishing from New York to Virginia. The societies had been introduced by immigrants from Ireland, a land Wesley had visited many times. (Before founding his first society, he had spent two years of his ministry in Georgia, a colony founded as a refuge for English debtors and other unfortunate individuals.)

The American Revolution almost wrecked the young church. Wesley in England wrote fiery pamphlets upholding King George III, thereby enraging the colonists. By 1778, seven of eight Wesleyan missionaries had to flee to England, leaving the embryo church of 15,000 members to the missionary Francis Asbury. An American nationalist, Asbury, by the war's end, had organized 83 preachers into 43 circuits. Then, in 1784, he called a conference in Baltimore to establish the first organized church in America independent of all foreign ties. Asbury himself assumed the title of Bishop, a move which infuriated Wesley, who had always intended that Methodist societies continue *within* the Church of England. At the inauguration of George Washington, Asbury and his co-superintendent Thomas Coke presented the new chief of state with a written pledge of allegiance. The Methodists thus became the first church to promise to support the new nation.

Early Methodists regarded their whole system as one big missionary endeavor. But official missionary efforts were begun at home in 1819 among the Wyandot Indians in Ohio, and abroad in 1832 in Africa.

Jason Lee, who stood a sinewy six-foot-three, accepted a call as missionary to the Flathead Indians of the Northwest in 1834. He soon began encouraging white settlement there, extolling Oregon as "the germ of a great state." It was Lee who, with others, drove a herd of cattle eighteen hundred miles from Independence, Missouri, to Oregon —along what came to be known as the Oregon Trail. Two years after his arrival, fearing that the United States meant to cede what is now both Oregon and Washington to Canada, Lee barnstormed his way East, exhorting everyone he met to head Northwest. He addressed Congress, personally recruited fifty-two new colonists for the Northwest and returned to Oregon with a gristmill and a printing press. Before the United States-Canada boundary treaty was signed, Lee had drafted a constitution for Oregon. He died at forty-one of tuberculosis contracted from overwork, and today is honored by statues both in Salem, Oregon, the state capital, and Washington, D. C.

In 1859, James M. Thoburn sailed for India. A member of the second Methodist mission to be sent there, he and his staff were to win no fewer than two hundred thousand converts to his cause. Not content with preaching, he also founded a chain of six English-language newspapers. After some ten years in the field, he wrote his sister Isabella, in Ohio, to join him.

He first put her to work at secretarial chores. One morning she disappeared, and was found teaching five Indian girls. Soon she was conducting regular classes, and a man with a club was stationed at her schoolroom door to repel any fathers who objected to such nonsense. Thoburn suggested she return to her secretarial work, but, with true Methodist stubbornness, she replied, "I have my own work to do." It was Isabella Thoburn who founded the influential college, named after herself, that was to become a leading woman's educational institution in India. Many of its graduates were to spark the movement for Indian independence from Great Britain.

Thoburn paved the way for such missionary giants as E. Stanley Jones, who entrenched the Methodist Church as the largest Protestant force in India. Indian Methodism today has four native bishops, and the Methodists in Pakistan have one. Growing nationalism among native Christians in other mission fields has led to the establishment of independent Methodist churches in Japan, Mexico, and Korea. (Apart from the giant United States church, Methodism today counts seven million followers in fifty lands.)

A Methodist missionary today little resembles Thoburn, who carved out a mission field for himself in India. The day of the lone ranger is past. So organized are foreign fields that Methodists send only highly trained specialists to supplement the work of native pastors. The new evangelists include architects and builders, pharmacists, dietitians, agronomists and theological instructors.

All are college graduates who must undergo rigorous physical and psychiatric examinations before embarking on their ministry. In 1957, the church sent 150 new career missionaries to join 1,500 in the field.

Outstanding among modern Methodist missionaries are Tom and Jennie Harris of Florida. Negroes, they are pioneers akin to Jackie Robinson in baseball. Harris is an agronomist and a former county farm agent; his wife is a schoolteacher. "With them," said the late Dr. Ralph Diffendorfer, secretary of the Methodist Mission Board, "we begin the work of our next hundred years."

In 1948, the Harrises were sent to Fukien Province, China; they were the first regularly commissioned Negro missionaries to be sent by any Christian church to an East Asian country. They did so splendidly there that when Chinese Communists over-ran the area, anti-American propaganda found no sympathizers among the villagers. The Harrises had disproved Communist charges that American Negroes were illiterate and exploited. They spoke fluent Chinese, had materially improved local agriculture and learning, and were friends to Chinese of the lowest stations.

Ordered out of China, they went to Sarawak, Borneo, in 1951 to work among the Dyaks. While Tom Harris taught his people how to double their yearly rice yield, his wife opened a school. Their Borneo mission is flourishing beyond the mission board's most optimistic hopes.

A social phenomenon back home initiated by Methodism was the "Great Revival" of the 1880's. It was sparked by a Methodist layman, John R. Mott, later known as the "grand old man of Methodism." Like other evangelical groups, Methodists had long believed that the business of church and religion was to deliver individual men from sin and spiritual death. But in a rapidly industrializing society, it was felt that something must also be done about the sins of society. Mott, who later was to win a Nobel Peace Prize, goaded churchmen into observing their religious duty in an era that worshiped business success. In a life-long crusade for interdenominational action, he was also a prime mover in the founding of the International Missionary Council and, in 1948, the World Council of Churches.

In preaching the "social gospel," Methodists since their beginning have gone after, and drawn the abuse of, entrenched privilege. In 1784, the first Methodist Discipline condemned slavery, a stand which provoked bitter quarrels within the church. Gradually, Methodism expanded its vision from the crusading of a few fearless radicals to a well-organized championship of civil and human rights. In 1908, Methodists issued their famous "Social Creed," which openly opposed sweatshops and child labor, favored labor unions, advocated the Golden Rule as the remedy for social ills. And in 1956, the General Conference voted that "planned parenthood, practiced in Christian conscience, may fulfill rather than violate the will of God."

Of all their campaigns, the Methodists' drive against liquor has been perhaps the most persistent. In 1873 a group of women (Methodist women are invariably ahead of their preachers in every crusade) knelt before saloon doors in Ohio and prayed for the destruction of liquor

traffic. The following year, they were leaders in the forma-
tion of the Woman's Christian Temperance Union. Frances
E. Willard, a Methodist who towered high in the suffra-
gette and anti-child-labor movements, became president
of the W.C.T.U. in 1879 and promptly expanded it into
a world organization.

In 1893, Methodist men got busy and dominated the
founding of the Anti-Saloon League, which throughout
its turbulent history has always counted at least one
Methodist bishop on its strategy board. Bishop James
Cannon, Jr., organizer of the Virginia Anti-Saloon League,
in 1928 opposed Al Smith, "a cocktail drinker and avowed
wet," for the Presidency. His campaign, which led Tennessee, Virginia, North Carolina, Florida and Texas into
the G.O.P. column, is credited by historians with breaking
the Democratic hold on the Solid South for the first time
since 1880. For this, among other things, he was attacked
as a bluenose and anti-Catholic bigot. The latter charge
perturbed Cannon most, and he took pains to prove that,
prior to Smith's nomination for the Presidency, he had
worked hard for the nomination of Senator Thomas J.
Walsh of Montana, a Catholic who favored Prohibition.
Incidentally, Carry Nation, the celebrated foe of alcohol,
arrested thirty times for breaking up saloons with a
hatchet, was a Free Methodist during her active career.

The Methodist Church's attitude toward alcohol
today is unrelenting but up-to-date. The Board of Temperance abets local-option elections which ban the selling
of alcoholic beverages. It supports Alcoholics Anonymous,
sponsors scientific studies of alcoholism and educates
youth with a barrage of films, seminars, workshops and

oratory. The board still asks young people to "take the pledge" not to drink, on Prohibition Sunday, now called Commitment Sunday. Where the old slogan was, "Lips that touch liquor shall never touch mine," the modern argument is that an alcohol-free way of life permits man to be the true master of himself.

The Methodists also have been militant pacifists. They were strong supporters of the League of Nations. When that effort failed with the Japanese invasion of Manchuria in 1931, the church was jolted to its roots. Immediately, a spontaneous campaign developed throughout world Methodism, galvanized by women and young people, to educate youth against war. By 1941, Methodists counted more conscientious objectors than any other big denomination, exceeded only by the so-called "peace churches," the Mennonites, the Brethren and the Quakers. It is significant that the Methodist Church never quite filled its assigned quota of World War II chaplains, though it worked hard in relief organizations.

When the Dumbarton Oaks Conference of 1944 set a new goal for world peace through a United Nations organization, the church endorsed it wholeheartedly. Its Crusade for a New World Order raised $27,000,000 to finance a drive led personally by seventy bishops. Every Methodist parish in America was deluged with leaflets. Speakers included national leaders from the late Wendell Willkie to Branch Rickey, then president of the Brooklyn Dodgers. Millions of prayers were offered for the success of the San Francisco Conference at which the United Nations was formed. Ever since, the Methodists have maintained two full-time observers at United Nations headquarters and handsomely supported the United Nations efforts of the National and The World Council of Churches.

On the Negro question, Methodism for ninety-five years was cleaved by a wound which has not yet entirely healed. A schism over the slavery issue split Northern and Southern Methodists into two churches in 1844, and the Methodist Episcopal Church, South, was formed in 1845.

In 1939, reunion finally took place, and 82 per cent of Methodism was at last united. The merger also created a segregated Central Jurisdiction, to minister to 3,000 all-Negro Methodist churches with a membership of 352,000. In some ways, this has worked to the Negroes' advantage, insuring them five bishops and automatic representation on every important church board and commission.

Discrimination is breaking down, however. As of 1956, more than 47,000 Negro members of the Methodist Church, as the merged body is called, had joined previously all-white conferences outside the Central Jurisdiction. At its 1956 conference, the church took its first constitutional step to liquidate the color line. However, 92 per cent of American Negro Methodists are still not affiliated with the merged body. Most of them belong to the African Methodist Episcopal Church, the African Methodist Episcopal Zion Church and the Christian Methodist Episcopal Church.

Methodist women, who in frontier days outnumbered male parishioners eight to one, have long interpreted St. Paul's declaration, "In Christ Jesus there is neither male nor female," to mean that women are not one whit inferior to men. In 1766, Barbara Heck, incensed on

catching her husband at card playing, implored a lay
preacher named Philip Embury to exhort him in their
home. It was the first Methodist meeting in New York
City. Joshua Monroe, sent to an Erie, Pennsylvania, circuit in 1810, found twenty-three of his twenty-four
preaching stations to be in private homes, where Methodist societies were nurtured by the ladies of the house. It
was Methodist women who packed missionary barrels,
organized Ladies Aid societies and hospitals, met to sew
and be "edified," and brought their errant husbands, by
the ear if necessary, to the meetinghouse. In time, these
dedicated women, banded into national bodies, became a
power to be reckoned with within the Methodist Church.
They were given the right to vote in church conferences
in 1904, fully sixteen years before national woman suffrage. A church conference in 1852 had debated the issue
to no avail, after which one bishop's wife would not speak
to her husband for five weeks.

With notable exceptions, Methodist men early took a
position that, since the word of God was inspired, no book
learning was required either to preach the Gospel or to
believe in it. But the women wanted their children educated, and it was the women who fed the circuit riders on
their rounds. Many a minister was won to the cause of
education through his stomach. Today United States
Methodism in all its branches has 139 schools, including
93 colleges and nine universities, in the United States
alone. The Woman's Society of Christian Service spends
more than $10,000,000 a year, and the church,
$101,000,000, to support hospitals, orphanages, homes
for the aged, settlement houses and educational insti-

tutions. About ten per cent of United States college students are enrolled in Methodist schools.

In 1956, women were finally given the right not only to be fully ordained Methodist preachers, but also to be members of the Annual Conferences which assign and supervise pastoral work. The milestone was reached with the acceptance to full ministerial duties of Mrs. Maud K. Jensen of Pennsylvania. At present, she is in Korea, carrying on the work of her late husband, Dr. Anders Kristian Jensen, who in 1953 was released after three years' captivity by the Chinese Communists. He died recently in Korea.

Methodists organized the first Sunday school in America in 1784, the first "Children's Day" in 1868 and the first national church youth club—the Epworth League—in 1880. They published a catechism, a simple primer on church beliefs, in 1824. A Methodist, Ann Jarvis, started Mother's Day at her church in Grafton, West Virginia. Today, 586,269 Methodist Sunday-school teachers teach nearly 7,000,000 pupils.

In the years 1880 to 1932, Methodism underwent a radical change. The descendents of humble pioneers had moved up the social ladder, to become respectable middle-class business and community leaders. Evangelistic zeal almost vanished from both the Methodist and Southern Methodist groups (though not from twenty-one smaller branches). The business meeting became more important than the prayer meeting. Great church edifices were built, and an Ohio survey made in 1920 showed that one-sixth of the poorer parishes had been abandoned. Far fewer "amens" and "hallelujahs" punctuated Methodist sermons, for the church's message had veered sharply away from a simple concern for salvation. Preachers were directing their appeals to the intellect rather than to the emotions.

The two big branches of Methodism lost thousands of adherents to the more fundamentalist Free Methodist, Wesleyan Methodist and Primitive Methodist churches, plus such other evangelistic bodies as the Church of the Nazarene, the Assemblies of God and the Seventh-day Adventists. In 1936 alone, seventy-two Methodist buildings fell under the sheriff's hammer and five thousand parishes were in "acute financial distress." However, the Depression jolted Methodism from its complacence of the 1920's. Concern grew because the church had virtually abandoned its traditional devotion to the poor and underprivileged, and because the Northern and Southern branches were harboring un-Christian prejudices against each other.

The merger of North and South in 1939 provided an impetus badly needed by the entire church. Total membership since 1940 has increased twenty-five per cent, while money contributions have rocketed from $75,608,-000 a year to $413,894,000.

Today, more than 250 churches a year are being built to minister to new communities. Churches in slum parishes are being revitalized. For some years after the war, mobile units scoured rural communities, recruiting the unchurched. In Nebraska, a trailer team traveled 35,000 miles in 18 counties, covering isolated villages which had heard no Methodist preaching for 15 years. More than 100 churches are thriving in American Indian settlements—a mission field which had become relatively inactive by the 1930's.

Parish members today knock on the door of un- churched families in their neighborhood, "exhort" unbe- lievers with logic if not with circuit-rider fervor and invite them to church. These efforts in essence are a throwback to the days when Methodists, in groups of two or three, invaded the homes of nonbelievers and persuaded them to see the light. In so doing, today's Methodists mightily revitalize their own faith as well as make converts. This "visitation evangelism," first employed during the worldly 1920's, has been used since World War II to recruit more than 250,000 new Methodists.

In short, the Methodists have taken a good hard look at themselves in the past ten years—a look John Wesley would approve. Everywhere Methodists are eval- uating themselves, casting off their bourgeois complacence and beginning to move with their traditional zealous spirit. To spur this soul-searching, they have revived an old Methodist couplet, with salutary effect. It goes like this:

If every church member were just like me,
What kind of a church would my church be?

2

The Baptists

ONE-THIRD OF ALL Protestants in America, one-half of all United States Negroes, more than one-fourth of all United States non-Roman Catholic church members are Baptists. For all their numbers, however, some Baptists do not consider their faith a denomination. There is no Baptist Church; there are only Baptist churches. Baptists recognize no human founder and no human spiritual authority. Some date their origin to the baptism of Jesus in the Jordan. Others contend, "We began with John Smyth in 1608."

Each local congregation is a law unto itself. No one can tell Baptists what to do, think or believe religiously—without having a fight on his hands. They are as independent as individuals can be. They have no formal creed, no sacraments, no set procedures for weddings or funerals. Although they are loosely organized into twenty-nine national associations, no one group has any general power: all may merely recommend ways in which like-minded Baptists can work together. As a result, there is wide variety in religious emphasis.

Some congregations such as the huge First Baptist Church, Los Angeles, and First Baptist Church, Dallas, feature oratorical preaching and missionary fund raising, while Primitive Baptists are opposed to modern mission-

23

ary societies. There are Baptists who attend church on
Saturday instead of Sunday, others whose uninhibited
emotionalism causes paroxysms and rolling in the church
aisles. There are northern Baptists, southern Baptists, all-
white Baptists, all-Negro Baptists, integrated Baptists and
foreign-language Baptists (at least eight tongues are represented). Specific names identify some of the groups.
They may be Free-Will, Seventh-day, Separate, Primitive,
Regular, General Six-Principle or Two-Seed-in-the-Spirit
Predestinarian. Regardless of their title, all are Baptists.

All told, Baptists number at least 20,000,000 in nearly
90,000 congregations in the United States, not including
several million in Sunday schools. No exact count is possible. Some associations carry on their rolls many with
whom they have lost contact; other tallies are incomplete,
since some groups decline to report their strength; others
merely make estimates. It is safe to say, however, that
there are about twice as many Baptists as Methodists, the
next largest non-Roman Catholic faith in America.

Within their diversity, there is remarkable unity on
certain fundamentals. The name "Baptist" stems from a
unanimous belief in baptism by total immersion. Baptists
reject infant baptism, holding that everyone baptized must
be old enough to make up his own mind about his religion.
They also maintain that every member is the equal,
socially and religiously, of every other. The pastor is
merely the leader of the flock, and his interpretations of
the Bible in sermons are not binding on his hearers, since
every Baptist must decide for himself what God is saying
to him through the Scriptures. The local church may "call"
anyone to be its pastor. Youths of fourteen have been so

inducted, and ordination at seventeen or eighteen is not
unusual among some groups.

The first tenet of all Baptists is that Jesus Christ is
the supreme authority, and that His purposes are revealed
only through the Bible. In matters of religion, no institution, tradition or dogma can dictate to a Baptist. In
Washington, D. C., the Baptist Joint Committee on Public
Affairs protests any violation or redefinition of the First
Amendment, any expenditure of public funds on religious
institutions, any diplomatic representation at the Vatican.

A Baptist church is immediately recognizable from its
interior. The auditorium makes no pretense of creating a
mystical atmosphere. It is dominated by a pulpit, to
accentuate the fact that preaching is all-important. The
preacher usually wears a business suit rather than a vest-
ment. Behind the choir, except in rural areas, is a bap-
tistry. This is a water tank about four feet deep. When
a new member is baptized, the preacher descends into
the water. (Some preachers wear rubber hip boots.) The
candidate is brought before him. The pastor, in the name
of the Trinity, immerses the candidate below the surface
of the water. This symbolizes both Christ's death and
resurrection and the burial of the sinner and his rebirth
as a Christian. When indoor baptistries are not available,
preachers lead their flocks to a river or shoreline and
immerse the candidates there.

Once every two or three months, each congregation
holds a business meeting. The entire membership partici-
pates, and matters affecting the congregation are settled
by majority vote. In practice, much routine is delegated to
the pastor, his deacons and sometimes a "cabinet" of

committee chairmen who are elected in open meeting. This personal voice in church affairs encourages participation in church work and loyalty to the cause.

Women are employed as preachers only in the North. The American Baptist Convention has approximately thirty, including one Negro. These women range from a grammar-school graduate to a Ph.D. Typical, perhaps, of the Baptist attitude toward women is the comment of one woman minister: "Two types of churches will consider a woman pastor. One is the broad-minded church; the other is the type too poor to hire a man. Since among Baptists there are none of the former, that leaves only the latter." In the South, women are not usually permitted to hold important Convention offices, except in the mission societies. Only five women have served on the Southern Baptist Convention's executive committee.

The word "Baptist" entered the English language through the leadership of two Englishmen, John Smyth and Thomas Helwys. They fled to the Netherlands to escape religious persecution, and founded the first Baptist congregation in 1609. Their followers supported Oliver Cromwell's fight against the established Church of England. The belief crystallized in America under Roger Williams.

Williams was the son of a prosperous London merchant tailor. As a Church of England priest, he united with the Puritan faction, which advocated simplicity and liberality of religious opinion. Because of his radical, outspoken views, he was given the choice of jail or banishment. He fled to the New World, reaching Boston in 1631.

But here he disagreed with the Puritan religious monopoly, the assessment of taxes to support Puritanism as the state church, and the use of civil law to enforce church punishments. He became such a nuisance to the Puritans that they, too, threatened to banish him. Rather than face deportation, Williams took refuge among the Narragansett Indians in 1636. From them, he secured the land where Providence, Rhode Island, now stands. The settlers of this new colony drew up a compact of government, submitting themselves to the law of the majority "only in civil things." Here, American liberties were for the first time defined and practiced; here, the pattern of American democracy was cut.

Roger Williams founded the first Baptist church in the New World. In 1639, he and a dozen friends baptized each other by immersion, united in a "soul liberty" congregation and established the First Baptist Church of Providence. Williams remained a Baptist for less than a year. He withdrew from the church he had founded, to become a Seeker, hoping to find a faith more congenial to his spiritual wants.

For sixty years, the group Williams founded met in private homes. The Baptists' first church building was at Newport, where a group of dissenters from Puritan Boston had settled. Their church, led by Dr. John Clarke, had adopted Baptist principles by 1644. As an envoy from Rhode Island to Charles II, Clarke negotiated a revised and more liberal charter for Rhode Island.

However, these events were only the start in the fight for religious self-determination. At the time, only Rhode Island, and to some extent three other colonies, permitted freedom of worship. State-supported churches existed in nine of the thirteen colonies, and dissenters were persecuted. No Baptists were martyrs to their belief, as were Quakers, but hundreds were jailed or beaten. One Baptist kept a meticulous list of these abuses and for thirty-nine years stumped from Maine to South Carolina, orating for religious freedom. His name was Isaac Backus.

Born in Norwich, Connecticut, in 1724, Backus joined the dissenters when his widowed mother was jailed for refusing to accept Puritanism. He rode 60,000 miles making speeches, wrote books and pamphlets, spoke for religious freedom before the Continental Congress and the Constitutional Convention. Backus preached that the church and state must never be united.

In his political maneuvering for constitutional guarantees, Backus was assisted by another Baptist preacher, John Leland, a Massachusetts man who went to Virginia to fight that colony's religious monopoly. He became a friend of Thomas Jefferson and James Madison, enlisting their support and strengthening their own convictions. Leland was determined to become a member of the Virginia convention called to ratify the United States Constitution. He wanted to force Backus's views into the document. In the Orange County election of a convention delegate, Leland was opposed by James Madison. Leland had the election won, and he knew it; but he also realized that Madison's was a more persuasive political voice. So the two met, at a site that is now known as the Leland-Madison State Park. There, Madison agreed to introduce an amendment to the Constitution assuring separation of church and state, if Leland would withdraw. Leland withdrew. The first of the ten amendments in the Bill of Rights contains the guarantee of freedom of religion.

From 1775 to about 1830, most Baptist preachers made annual tours, during which they rode hundreds of miles to hold revivals or camp meetings, to enlist new followers and to establish new churches. A few congregations literally transplanted themselves, becoming known to Baptist history as "traveling churches." One such congregation migrated en masse from Kittery, Maine, to Charleston, South Carolina, in 1684, where it established the first Baptist church in the South.

The first Protestant church in the Northwest Territory was the Columbia Baptist Church, founded in 1789 by Major Benjamin Stites, at what today is Cincinnati, Ohio. Missionaries greatly spurred Baptist growth. In 1832, Isaac McCoy, one of the most famous Indian missionaries, founded the first Baptist church in the Indian Territory, at Ebenezer Station in the Creek (Muskogee) Nation. Jesse Bushyhead, a pioneer Cherokee Indian leader in Oklahoma, was a Baptist preacher. The first newspaper of any kind published in Oklahoma was the *Cherokee Messenger,* sponsored by the Baptist Missionary Society in Boston. Northern Baptists, in 1849, sent Hiram W. Read to Santa Fe, New Mexico, as a missionary, the earliest resident Baptist worker in that state. Daniel Boone's brother was the first Baptist preacher to settle on Kentucky soil, in 1776. Abraham Lincoln's father helped erect a log-cabin Baptist meetinghouse at Pigeon Creek, Indiana, in 1819.

Baptists also were a vital force in Texas's independence. They fought because Mexico refused them public worship and forcibly closed their Sunday schools. Active in the uprising was Noah T. Byars, who owned a blacksmithy at Washington-on-the-Brazos. In his shop were written both the Texas Declaration of Independence and the Constitution of the Texas Republic. At these historic meetings, another leader was Baptist lawyer Richard Ellis, who presided over the convention at which the independence of Texas was proclaimed. Robert E. B. Baylor, an ordained Baptist, was a member of the Texas Republic's supreme court and a founder of Baylor University. Sam Houston, commander of Texas forces at San Jacinto and president of Texas, was also a Baptist.

During their growing years, frontier Baptists divided and reformed repeatedly in their refusal to be regimented. If a majority of one congregation voted to adopt some new-fangled notion, the minority would secede and create a new congregation. In the Tennessee backwoods, a group calling itself the "Do Me Good" Baptists split on the question of whether to support missionaries. The dissenters packed up, went a mile down the road and set up a church which they called "Do Me Better."

The first American Protestant overseas missionary was a Baptist. In 1812, Adoniram Judson and Luther Rice had sailed for India as Congregational missionaries. Converted to Baptist belief en route, Judson went on to Burma, and Rice returned to organize support for the venture.

So vehemently did the rank and file resist regimentation of any degree that it was 1814 before a general convention for foreign missions was organized, but with the precise qualification that participation was purely voluntary and involved no denominational implications. By the following year, practically all of the 115 associations were able to co-operate, in what became known as the Triennial Convention, because it met every three years. On this pattern, other societies followed, for home missions and publications. When the Triennial Convention split in 1845, Northern and Southern Baptists continued their work independently.

Baptists are missionaries at heart. Their faith compels them to proclaim the Gospel, both at home and abroad. Since their preachers are no higher in God's sight than any member, it behooves everyone to "witness" for his faith, even though he can work no farther away than the corner supermarket. The two largest missionary efforts are provided by the all-white Southern Baptist Convention, with 8,966,255 members, and the American Baptist Convention, a Northern society of 1,536,275 constituents. In 1957, the Southerners raised over $9,000,000 for missions; the Northerners, more than $3,000,000. These sums support foreign missions and other world-wide activities.

At home, Baptist missionary work is as varied as the Baptists themselves. Many home-mission societies, sponsored by various groups, cover every possible aspect of evangelism in the United States. The scope of their work is remarkable. In Texas alone, the Southern Baptist Convention's members support 325 Spanish-speaking churches. The American Baptist Convention works zealously among American Indians in seven states. The Negro conventions concentrate on improving the social and religious life of their own race, but the white conventions work among Negroes, too, with particular emphasis on education and pastor training.

In the North, where more than half the members of the American Baptist Convention reside in cities of more than 10,000 population, the Baptists have attacked the social problems of the slums. Pastors go onto the streets and into the courtroom to combat juvenile delinquency. They work with irresponsible parents. Team ministries, including social workers, support hundreds of churches in congested areas, providing Christian centers for recreation, personal counseling and family help, as well as the usual religious services. Special heed is given to often-neglected groups, such as Orientals, war brides, refugees and immigrants, and draftees after their discharge. Institutionally, Baptists support more than 150 hospitals, homes for the aged and refuges for orphans and the victims of broken homes.

The modern "social-gospel" movement, which has had powerful impact on most churches, began with Walter Rauschenbusch, a Baptist preacher who worked in New York City's slums from 1886 to 1897, then became a teacher and writer. He astounded his Baptist colleagues when he asserted that saving individual souls was not enough; that the economic soul of society must be reborn to improve the social order. This gave new direction to Baptist home missions, particularly in such broad fields as labor-management relations, the improvement of working conditions and slum clearance.

The Baptists have been called "the church of the common people." It appeals mainly to the masses. More than half the Baptists are manual workers, 20 per cent are farmers. These economic groups also tend to have less education. In some Baptist bodies, the clergy is not much better educated than the laity. The two huge societies of Negro Baptists, the National Baptist Convention, United States of America, Inc., which claims to have about 4,557,000 members, and the National Baptist Convention of America, which embraces approximately 2,668,000, have 26,500 preachers, of whom it is estimated five per cent have been theologically trained. Among white Southerners, 62 per cent have finished college, but 20 per cent are not high-school graduates.

Since their beginnings in America, Baptists have offered their members a better education. Brown University, in Providence, Rhode Island, though now non-sectarian, was founded by Baptists in 1764. A Baptist founded Vassar in 1861. The Baptists also launched the universities of Chicago, Colgate and Rochester, among other institutions that no longer have a Baptist affiliation. The sixty-three Baptist-affiliated senior colleges today include Bucknell, Wake Forest, Furman, Richmond, Red-lands, Denison, and Baylor. In addition, there are many junior colleges, academies and special training schools. The twenty-six preacher-training seminaries maintained by Baptists include some of the best in Protestantism.

In public life, Baptists are well represented. They have fourteen United States senators and fifty-five representatives. They have produced dozens of state governors, two United States Presidents (Warren G. Harding and Harry S. Truman), a labor leader (the late AFL president, William Green) and a chief justice of the Supreme Court

(Charles Evans Hughes). Huey Long, the Louisianan whose slogan was "Every man a king," was a Baptist too.

A Baptist, Brigadier General Robert P. Taylor, is deputy chief of Air Force chaplains, and Brigadier General Frank A. Tobey, a Baptist, has been nominated to succeed Major General Patrick J. Ryan as chief of Army chaplains.

The celebrated Baptist preachers of today are as much in contrast as the calmly logical Harry Emerson Fosdick, of national radio fame, the emotional evangelist Billy Graham and controversial Representative Adam Clayton Powell of Harlem's Abyssinian Baptist Church. Most of the Southern backwoods people are Baptist, but so are the Rockefellers in New York.

An English Baptist, William Fox, organized the first Sunday-school society in 1785. The first Sunday-school paper in the United States, *The Young Reaper,* was Baptist. The famous Uniform Sunday School Lessons were developed by a Chicago Baptist layman, B. F. Jacobs, and a Methodist preacher, J. H. Vincent.

Another Baptist, Benjamin F. White, preserved many of the old gospel songs in a book, *Sacred Harp.* For those unable to read music, he employed a recognition system using four notes of different shapes. Shape-note song books still sell more than a million copies a year.

Almost all Baptists, old and young, attend Sunday school, held for an hour before the morning church service. The Baptist sermon is often highly emotional. Preachers inveigh against alcohol, gambling, dance halls, immoral books and movies, bathing-beauty contests and, in some sections, social dancing.

There is also a preaching service on Sunday night and a midweek prayer meeting, often preceded by supper. This Wednesday service may feature testimonials, in which members tell how God has helped them personally. All the sick are reported on and prayed for.

At the moment, many prayers are being offered for the race-integration problem. But there is no unanimity on how these prayers should be answered. That there should be racial conflict is contrary to the Baptists' avowed belief that every Baptist is the equal of every other. The problem is not one-sided. The two big all-Negro societies are as adamant against corporate merger as are some of the Southern whites. They fear that their particular social concerns and needs would be swamped by the emphatic white leadership.

Since every congregation is independent, the members of a Baptist society may rationalize any position. Fifteen white Baptist ministers called a prayer meeting for peace through segregation during the Little Rock school crisis of 1957, while four others attended a "reconciliation" prayer service. There are white Baptist ministers in the South who publicly assert that the Bible favors segregation. On the other side, a white Baptist preacher was beaten while escorting Negro children to an integrated school at Clinton, Tennessee.

In the North, at least twenty per cent of all American Baptist Convention churches have Negro members, and the Convention itself is approaching the issue directly with a church program that suggests, "Attack the problem, not the people." Although the Southern Baptist

Convention has been called "a silent but powerful accessory to the segregation pattern," actually it has been on record since 1947 with a resolution that states, "We shall think of the Negro as a person and treat him accordingly," and urges education as a means of eliminating racial prejudice.

There are some integrated Baptist churches and schools in Texas, Arizona, Oklahoma, Missouri and Kentucky, but none in the "black belt" of Mississippi, Georgia, Florida, Louisiana, Alabama, Arkansas and South Carolina. All the seminaries of the Southern Baptist Convention will accept Negro students.

Before the Civil War, Southern Baptist churches had no discrimination; both slaves and free Negroes were admitted to membership. One of the first Negro missionaries from the United States, Lott Cary, was sent to Africa in 1821 by the Baptist General Convention. The Circular Church of Charleston, South Carolina, had four hundred Negro members in 1804, and the First Baptist Church of Montgomery, Alabama, numbered six hundred Negroes to three hundred whites in 1865. One of the most celebrated Southern Baptist pioneer preachers was John Jasper, born a slave in 1812. He preached his famous sermon, "The Sun Do Move," at least two hundred and fifty times. This sermon included the question, "How in de name of God can de earth be roun' when de Bible speak of its four corners?"

This happy mutuality of the races was destroyed in the frictions that led to the Civil War, causing the secession of Southern Baptists from the Triennial Convention in 1845 to organize the Southern Baptist Convention. But not until after the war, when the South lay prostrate, were Southern Negroes and whites finally committed to organization along color lines. The Negroes were abetted by the army of occupation. Since then, the white Southern Baptists have gone their own way. But they have liberally supported the Negro groups. Baptists' care of the freed slaves is the chief reason why so many Negroes today are Baptists.

Old frictions chafe the major issue. Baptists know their own minds, and their tradition causes them to speak out bluntly. They have never feared either man or government, and they are not going to be pushed around on any issue—not even by the United States Supreme Court. There is also a conflict of interest between the English-stock rural South and the many-race, urbanized North. There are sophisticated theological emphases in the North that the more fundamentalist Southerners cannot accept. There are differences in music and dialect, and strong personal rivalries of denominational leaders, particularly among Negro groups.

But, despite many conflicts, the Baptists move ahead. Their number increased 243 per cent from 1906 to 1956. Baptist growth is so phenomenal that, at a recent interdenominational rally, Methodist Bishop G. Bromley Oxnam quipped he had been informed by a Southern Baptist statistician that "if the present rate of growth continues, there would be more Southern Baptists than people by the year 2015." The Baptists liked that. They look upon themselves as unusual, as true Christians and not just as people.

The reason for the Baptists' growth is simple: They work at it. "We are one vast missionary enterprise," says Dr. Reuben E. Nelson, general secretary of the American Baptist Convention, referring to all Baptist groups. Currently, the six largest conventions, both white and Negro, are teamed on a five-year Jubilee Advance, during which ambitious targets have been set up to expedite Baptist work in every field, from missions and education to race relations. The Southern Baptist Convention alone hopes to develop 10,000 new churches and 20,000 new preaching stations or missions. It estimates that there are some 55,000,000 unchurched whites in the United States, and it is out to enroll all of them. In 1955, the Southerners held simultaneous revival meetings in most of their 30,797 churches. The result was 416,816 baptisms. Due to this success, the Convention-wide revival has become an annual event.

The Baptists want everybody to be as conscious of them as was the twenty-year-old secretary who recently went to a Dallas bank to get some traveler's checks. "What denomination?" asked the teller. "Why, Baptist, of course," she replied.

Many Baptists who don't agree that they are a denomination might question her terminology, but they would know what she meant. She was a Baptist—and proud of it.

3

The Lutherans

A N EXTRAORDINARY TRANSFORMATION in the past few years has been rapidly changing the character and size of the Lutheran churches and synods of America.

For three hundred years, most of the Lutheran churches in this country could be identified by their European origin. They were German, Swedish, Norwegian, Danish, Slovak, or Finnish. But this is not the case today. Throughout the country, Lutherans are shedding their foreign characteristics and are rearing in the suburbs hundreds of new edifices in which the worshipers are as polyglot in background as the nation itself.

The Lutherans exemplify the present revival of religious interest. During 1946-56, they increased by 1,716,-592 (in 1956, their total United States membership was 7,388,176). This gain is comprised primarily of converts who have found in the clear-cut, uncompromising doctrines of Martin Luther, founder of the Reformation, a message suited to modern needs.

Lutheran theology contains nothing new-fangled, nothing sensational. It is based squarely on New Testament Gospel, and on the thesis that man is naturally sinful, constantly in need of Christ's forgiving grace. After two world wars and an apparently universal moral collapse, Lutheran pastors need little documentation for the argument that sin is always with us, and that the New Testament teaching of the salvation of man through Christ is the answer to today's religious uncertainty.

The new converts have not, however, just walked in the door. They have been recruited by brisk, up-to-the-minute methods. With imagination and fervor, the Lutherans have adapted twentieth-century techniques to Gospel preaching. New congregations are organizing at the rate of one every 54 hours; their new churches are so ultramodern in architecture that they are the talk of their communities. The Lutherans have the biggest program on radio, a weekly network sermon on 1,250 stations. They preach in one-act parable plays to 9,000,000 television viewers a week. They advertise nationally on billboards. They catch the ear with new polyphonic church music, the eye with brilliant interior decoration, the senses with perfect acoustics, electronic marvels and dramatic liturgies. With a canny sense of practicality, they even provide parking space for everybody's automobile. And through a campaign of "Preaching, Teaching, Reaching," they have set their lay men and women to knocking on every door in their neighborhoods, inviting the unchurched and the religiously unsatisfied to join them in finding the answers to life's perplexities.

This evangelistic surge is of rather recent origin. The entire denomination has come alive, as though it had suddenly decided to make good President Theodore Roosevelt's fifty-three-year-old prophecy that "the Lutheran Church is destined to become one of the two or three greatest and most important churches in the United States. . . ."

Lutheran leaders began to realize that the denomination could not grow if it concentrated only on the descendants of Scandinavian and German settlers, as it had done in the past. Originally, such a limitation was necessary, for until the present century, worship services and sermons were chiefly in a foreign tongue. Indeed, the old-fashioned Norwegian-speaking pastor could not even proselyte among the Germans; he did not speak their language. But foreign services are limited today, directed to new immigrants and the older generation. Most congregations use English alone, and are able to welcome anyone. However, some older pastors resist the change. An upstate New York minister, for example, urged to organize a doorbell campaign for new members, said, "It would be a waste of time; there are no unchurched Swedes here." In northern Wisconsin, a Norwegian pastor revealed his irritation with the new order. Reporting to his synod on a drive for non-Norwegian converts, he wrote, "We have here sixty-seven Christians and one Swede."

But such attitudes are unusual. The Lutherans have zealously organized congregations in the new suburbs. This emphasis is so pronounced that some pastors have been moved to paraphrase the Beatitudes and say, "Blessed are the Lutherans who move to the suburbs, for they shall be saved."

The Lutherans themselves are amazed at the success of their appeal to the unchurched. They are astounded at their own audacity after generations of shy Scandinavian reticence and stubborn German aloofness. But they are by no means agreed that all of what is happening is good. The Lutherans of America are divided into 16 separate bodies. Some of them are called synods —a term meaning governing or advisory body; others are designated as churches. The more conservative groups are anxious lest the "new" Lutherans undermine the faith. Powerful leaders of less conservative groups, like Dr. Franklin Clark Fry, president of the Lutheran World Federation and also of the United Lutheran Church, with 2,243,946 United States-baptized members, and Dr. F. Eppling Reinartz, president of the National Lutheran Council, are supremely confident of the future. They each travel about 50,000 miles a year, make hundreds of speeches and preside at dozens of conferences, urging Lutherans to spring even more actively into national religious leadership. With equal zeal, the leaders of the Missouri Synod, with 2,078,227 United States members, argue the necessity for making haste slowly to preserve the "pure" Lutheran doctrine.

Thus a great controversy has arisen, in which the entire church membership has taken sides. Paradoxically, this dispute is not dividing the Lutherans, but driving them closer together. By 1965, mergers now in process will reorganize the sixteen present churches and synods in America into ten, and these into three main groups, the ultraconservatives, the conservatives and the comparatively liberal. (Theologically speaking, there is no such thing as a "liberal" Lutheran.)

Lutherans thrive on dispute. The Ohio and Iowa synods debated doctrinal differences for fifty years, amid bitter name calling, and then happily merged. President

T. O. Burntvedt of the Lutheran Free Church observed a few years ago that the Lutherans had less to divide them, yet more greatly magnified their almost invisible differences, than the members of any other faith. Another leading churchman recently commented facetiously, "We Lutherans not only argue such ridiculous propositions as how many angels can dance on the point of a needle, but we dispute whether an angel should be dancing at all." Some Lutherans even refuse to admit they are Protestants. The magazine *The American Lutheran* stated editorially in October, 1956, that there are actually four religious faiths in the United States: Protestant, Roman Catholic, Jewish and Lutheran.

The Lutheran Church is the largest Protestant body in the world, numbering 70,770,000 persons, or almost three per cent of the world's population. A giant international rally, the Lutheran World Federation, was held in August, 1957, in Minneapolis. Delegates attended from almost every nation in the world. They included several from behind the Iron Curtain, among them Bishop Lajos Ordass of Hungary. Like the late Roman Catholic Josef Cardinal Mindszenty, Ordass is an international symbol of the resistance of free peoples to communism. He spent twenty months in prison for refusing to surrender his church to Communist influence.

In the United States, the Lutheran denomination now ranks fourth in size, behind the Roman Catholics, the Baptists and the Methodists. As most Americans know from the popular motion picture *Martin Luther,* which was produced with Lutheran support in 1952, the Lutheran Church is the church of the Reformation. Martin Luther was an Augustinian monk who taught theology at the University of Wittenberg in Saxony. On October 31, 1517, he nailed on the door of the Castle Church in Wittenberg a document containing ninety-five protests against certain Catholic practices.

This defiance of the Pope occurred at a time when nationalism was rising throughout Europe. Many princes and merchants had found Papal authority frustrating to their own ambitions, as had many peasants and others, who were then breaking with feudalism. Luther had no intention of founding a church. He merely wished to start a reform within the Catholic faith. But public excitement over his dramatic defiance stirred controversy all over Europe. In defending himself, Luther broadened his position and challenged many Catholic practices. Finally, after years of debate and armed warfare, the German princes threw off allegiance to Rome and organized Protestant churches on Luther's model. Sweden espoused the Reformation in 1527; Denmark followed in 1536, and Norway and Iceland soon thereafter. Thus, in all these countries, Lutheranism was bound to national as well as to religious sympathies.

Luther placed great emphasis on the individual's direct responsibility to God. Every believer, Luther argued, was in effect a priest, and could reach God directly by prayer, without the intercession of ordained ministers or saints. Though man was naturally wicked and prone to sin, he could be saved by faith in Christ, who by His death on the Cross had atoned for the sins of all men.

Consequently, faith is all-important; good works cannot wipe out evil deeds. Luther's theology made men free to read the Bible, to interpret Scripture, to participate by song and response in the worship service. It also removed the mystic function of the priest, and placed him in the role of pastor and servant of the congregation.

The basic tenets of Lutheranism were drawn together in 1530 by Philip Melanchthon, a German theologian and colleague of Luther's, in collaboration with Luther. This document was submitted to the Diet of Augsburg, and has been known since as the Augsburg Confession. It is the bedrock of American Lutheran belief, to which United States Lutherans have added an implacable opposition to any union, or in some synods even co-operation, between church and state.

The first Lutherans to settle in the American colonies were Dutch merchants, who reached New Amsterdam in 1624. The first Swedish Lutherans established a colony in 1638 at Fort Christina (now Wilmington) on the Delaware River; the next year, the Reverend Reorus Torkillus became the first regular Lutheran minister in America. It fell to Swedish settlers on Tinicum Island, near Philadelphia, to build the first Lutheran church in 1646. The Reverend Johan Campanius, sent by the Swedish Church as chaplain to the colony of New Sweden, translated Luther's Small Catechism into an Indian dialect. This was the first Protestant translation for Indians in America.

When William Penn arrived in 1682 to found Philadelphia, he selected a site on which Swedish Lutherans had been settled for forty-four years. Penn was so impressed by the Lutheran policy of friendship with the Indians that he adopted it. When he signed his famous treaty of amity with the natives, his interpreter was a Swedish Lutheran, Lawrence Kock.

Jonas Bronck, a Dane, arrived in New Amsterdam in 1639 and soon after purchased five hundred acres of what is today one of the world's most valuable parcels of real estate—the Bronx, which was named for him. His fine stone house contained the first private library in New York.

Perhaps the most famous pre-Revolutionary Lutheran was John Peter Zenger. He was one of three thousand Germans who sought religious freedom in a body, migrating here in 1710. In 1733, he established a newspaper, the *New York Weekly Journal,* which sharply criticized British colonial administration. When he was jailed for sedition, his friends hired a noted trial lawyer, Andrew Hamilton, for the defense. Despite instructions by the judge to condemn Zenger, the jury found him not guilty. Thus Zenger was responsible for the first important victory for freedom of the press in America.

Between 1700 and the Revolution, thousands of Lutherans migrated from the German states. Many were uprooted from their homes by the religious wars that accompanied the Reformation. Others were unable to accept changes made in the Augsburg Confession by German princes to advance their own nationalistic aims. In their new home, the migrants opposed state religion in any form. They settled chiefly in rural areas along the Delaware and Susquehanna rivers, in the fertile mountain valleys that have become known as the "Pennsylvania Dutch" country, and more sparsely in Virginia and the Carolinas.

A typical colony of these early eighteenth-century arrivals was made up of ninety-one families who established a home twenty miles up the Savannah River. In 1731, the Lutherans of Salzburg, Austria, were given the choice of embracing the Roman Catholic faith or of being expelled. These families chose their religion—and Georgia. Their house of worship on Ebenezer Island, called Jerusalem Church, is one of the few public buildings that remain in Georgia today from colonial times.

All these Germans brought their own form of Lutheranism with them, and relied on the mother churches for support and inspiration for many years. Each group had leaders who were men of learning and substance. After 1750, about eighty-five per cent of the Lutheran arrivals were literate. A flamboyant Lutheran of this period was Henry William Stiegel, called "the Baron" because of his ostentation. A German from Manheim, Stiegel established in Lancaster County, Pennsylvania, a factory from which came the finest glassware in colonial America. Stiegel, incidentally, gave to the Zion Lutheran Church in Manheim, Pennsylvania, the site for a building. He stipulated a rental of one red rose per year, a charge still paid in a ceremony each June.

So scattered were the Lutherans, and so few their pastors, that the denomination probably would have perished except for the work of Henry Melchior Muhlen-

berg, a Saxon who arrived in 1742, at the age of thirty-
one. He soon discovered that only about one-seventh of
the Lutheran settlers had become active church members.
Also, in three Pennsylvania towns, Muhlenberg was
forced to oust unordained impostors who were fraud-
ulently ministering to the Lutheran congregations. Supporting himself by giving music lessons and by selling
medicines, Muhlenberg traveled thousands of miles on
horseback to organize the isolated Lutheran settlements.
He also educated fifty young men for the ministry in
his own home and insisted that schools be erected in
every parish, to train pastors and lay leaders.

In 1748, Muhlenberg's organization, "The United
Pastors," became the nucleus of a united American
Lutheranism, and a tiny church, independent of European ties, was born. By 1765, Muhlenberg was the
foremost Lutheran leader between New York and Virginia, having banded 15,000 members of the faith into
133 flourishing congregations. More than half the
parishioners were farmers, the remainder chiefly weavers,
millers, tradesmen and artisans in little towns. The
laymen, in the absence of preachers, had become leaders
of the church. Wisely, Muhlenberg recognized their
contribution. In his constitution for member churches,
he made each congregation independent, controlled by
its own members; the synod had no authority except
that specifically delegated by each parish. To this day,
that pattern is followed throughout Lutheranism in
America.

Muhlenberg also gave to America two leaders of the
Revolution—his own sons. In so doing, he established
a precedent that Lutheran pastors do not mix politics

and religion. His sons, John Peter and Frederick, were both pastors. Their father, though revolutionary in spirit, permitted no political sermons, adhering to Luther's own belief that the pulpit should be reserved for theology and the Gospel. John Peter was stationed in Virginia's Shenandoah Valley at the outbreak of war. On a January Sunday in 1776, he conducted his service as usual and pronounced the benediction. Then, dramatically, he cast off his black ministerial robe, revealing himself in the uniform of a Continental Army colonel. "There is a time for all things," he said, "a time to preach and a time to fight, and now is the time to fight." He called for volunteers for the Eighth Virginia Regiment. By nightfall, he had recruited three hundred men. But he was careful to send his clergyman's certificate to his father, thus resigning from the ministry. John Peter rose to the rank of major general, and after the war became a representative and then a senator from Pennsylvania.

Meanwhile, his brother Frederick, not to be eclipsed, surrendered his pastoral certificate and set out to use his oratorical powers for the Revolutionary cause. He was a member of the Continental Congress and the first speaker of the United States House of Representatives. To this day, Lutheran pastors who embark on political activity deposit their ministerial credentials with their synod presidents. The latest such case was that of Joseph Simonson, President Eisenhower's appointee as ambassador to Ethiopia from 1953 to 1957. On his release from his post, Simonson was reinstated to the ministry and later accepted a call to a Lutheran church in Superior, Wisconsin.

The Lutherans were excellent soldiers in the Revolution. Entire male congregations joined the Continental Army in a body. One such company, the famous German Fusiliers, was recruited entirely from the Lutheran congregation in Charleston, South Carolina. John Adam Treutlen of Georgia was the Army's quartermaster general; Bodo Otto of Philadelphia, its surgeon general of hospitals; Christopher Ludwig of Pennsylvania, its baker general. In Maryland, John Hanson, a Swede, vigorously helped organize the colonies in defiance of the Stamp Act. He then recruited troops in his home state. Hanson is often called "the first president of the United States," since he was elected president of the Continental Congress of 1781.

Henry Melchior Muhlenberg's work continued after his death in 1787. His dream of a theological seminary, to give Lutherans adequate numbers of native-born pastors, took shape in 1815 in Hartwick, New York. Later, in 1826, the first official seminary was founded at Gettysburg, Pennsylvania, where, in the first 40 years, 500 men were trained for the ministry. By 1823, there were 45,000 Lutherans in America. State synods were being organized, and a loose attempt at federation existed in the General Synod, founded in 1820. However, the "old-country" legacy was strong, with different accents, both lingual and theological, making compact organization impossible. After 1850, there were 150 different Lutheran synods.

The most famous of the later migrations concerned the fathers of the Missouri Synod. A group of 760

Saxons sold all their belongings, pooled $88,000 and moved in a body to St. Louis, Missouri, arriving in 1839. They purchased 4,475 acres of land in Missouri's Perry County, and settled down with thousands of books, several pianos, an organ and instruments for a full orchestra. Leadership of the colony soon settled on Carl F. W. Walther, a 29-year-old organizational genius who guided his fellows with resolute determination for the next 47 years. In 1847, Walther established the conservative Missouri Synod, which even today declines to worship with the almost two-thirds of the nation's Lutherans who affiliate with less conservative bodies, until agreement on doctrine has been reached. However, the synod is co-operating with other Lutheran bodies in service to the armed forces, refugee resettlement and world relief.

Entire towns in Missouri, Illinois and other Mississippi Valley localities, during Walther's day, remained solidly German until the influx of population and growing missionary work changed them. The Church was vigorously opposed to those transplanted elements of German culture that were not consonant with the new America and with religious belief. Since Martin Luther had translated the Bible into German, and since the Augsburg Confession was German in origin, a small minority resisted the change to English-language worship services and instruction in the Church's parochial schools. Before he died in 1887, Walther saw his little Missouri Synod expand to 1,500 congregations with 300,000 members in 24 states. Today, the church body annually contributes the largest number of new members to American Lutheranism, the majority of whom are adult converts.

Meanwhile, the upper Midwest was similarly dominated by Scandinavians. Beginning about 1830, large numbers of Norwegians, Swedes and Danes settled in Wisconsin, Minnesota, Iowa, Illinois, Michigan and the Dakotas. They were all Lutheran in background, although fewer than 30 per cent of them were affiliated with the Church. Between 1870 and 1910, more than 1,750,000 Scandinavians migrated to the upper Mississippi Valley, and by 1910, Minnesota alone had more than 1,000,000 Northmen.

The Scandinavian Lutherans were a pious people who stressed family prayers, fireside Scripture readings and grace at table. They were so honest that their handshake was enough security for any business deal. They were so frugal that they would not light the candles on the altar except on Communion Sundays, and then not until the offertory hymn. And they were great singers.

Luther himself had emphasized the value of music, which he called "an inexpressible miracle of the Lord." He sang well and played the lute and the flute. He appreciated the inspirational value of choral music. To encourage hymn singing, he collaborated on the first Protestant hymnal, which included four of his own compositions. His towering hymn, "A Mighty Fortress Is Our God," is often called "The Battle Hymn of the Reformation." He also composed choir music based on the Gospel stories, thus anticipating the eighteenth-century Lutheran genius, Johann Sebastian Bach, and his contemporary, George Frederick Handel.

Music, therefore, is second nature to Lutherans. They are proud to belong to "the singing church." This emphasis led the Saint Olaf College choir, in Northfield, Minnesota, to create a new standard for choral groups and glee clubs throughout the United States with its *a cappella* polyphonic singing. The late F. Melius Christiansen, director of the group, composed or arranged two hundred choral compositions now in general use.

The Midwest today is overlaid with German and Scandinavian Lutheran influences. Sociologically, the area is marked by strong family ties, literacy, honesty, a low crime rate, a faithful church attendance and ethical businessmen. Politically, it tends to isolationism and distrust of big business and big government. Its people respond little to spellbinders, mind their own business, resist fads and innovations. The Good Samaritan spirit and a strong sense of community are Midwestern characteristics. All these are in Lutheranism's heritage from its founder.

Socially, the Lutherans tend to be independent farmers and good burghers, interested chiefly in their own affairs. A survey made in 1956, by the predominantly Midwestern synod known as the American Lutheran Church, indicated that 25,000 of its communicants held public office. Lutherans believe, as did their founder, in the dignity of hard work. Another survey showed that more than half the members were farmers. In the cities, skilled labor predominated. Lutherans have more members in United States labor unions than any other denomination except the Roman Catholic.

The high standards of public education in the Midwest have been supported enthusiastically by the Scandinavian Lutherans. They demanded—and got—the best for their children, following Luther's insistence that every man must be both literate and a thinker. Before the introduction of public schools in America, the Lutherans operated 400 elementary institutions. Today, they are the chief Protestant supporters of parochial schools, with 1,460 elementary institutions serving 133,731 students. Of these, 80 per cent are operated by members of the Missouri Synod. In addition, there are 32 senior colleges with 32,338 students, plus high schools and junior colleges enrolling 12,058, and 23 theological seminaries with 3,344 students.

The Lutherans came of age during the two world wars. Previously, they had tended to look for inspiration to the mother churches of Europe that had fostered them. Now, suddenly, they discovered that these parent churches desperately needed help. About two-thirds of the American synods pooled $2,700,000 and their talents for relief work, principally in Germany, after World War I. In addition, they sent abroad about $4,000,000 in used clothing. During the war, a National Lutheran Council had been organized to minister to Lutherans in the services. This council was broadened into an executive agency to handle relief.

But the great call on American Lutherans came after World War II. The Lutheran relief and resettlement achievement was one of the largest church-directed humanitarian efforts in Protestant history. The American churches began to plan their program before the war's end, since the greatest destruction was in Germany, an area with a huge Lutheran population. UNRRA could help only refugees and DPs, not German nationals.

For two years, the Lutherans were almost on their own in helping these nationals. Nearly every Lutheran congregation in America contributed to European relief. Youth clubs engaged in scavenger hunts for clothing. Tiny tots assembled "kiddy kits" containing crayons, soap and layettes. Grain, dairy products and meat from Lutheran farms, worth $1,500,000, were donated in three years.

Before this need had subsided, the Lutherans turned to the task of providing new homes for displaced persons, in co-operation with Church World Service and the United Nations. The Lutheran contribution to this purpose was $3,462,000 in cash and new homes for 38,254 refugees. American Lutherans also gave $26,000,000 in postwar interchurch aid for Europe, Asia, Africa, and Latin America. Their total war-relief effort, in all its phases, cost $50,000,000 in cash, plus $77,500,000 in supplies.

During this service, the Lutherans learned to co-operate with government agencies. The United States Government transported free all the Lutheran war-rescue supplies, despite the tradition that Lutherans must not embroil themselves with government.

Martin Luther's Reformation, by emphasizing the doctrine of "the priesthood of all believers," placed great responsibility on Lutheran laymen. The present evangelistic drive of all American Lutheran bodies is often lay-inspired. By the time the theologians have searched

Scriptures and Luther's writings for a precedent, the laymen frequently have the task under way.

A good example of this is the Missouri Synod's vast use of radio. This was begun by the Lutheran Laymen's League, an organization distinct from the synod but composed entirely of synod laymen. They wanted to use the airwaves to prove to all America that Lutherans could speak the English language as well as anybody else, and that, as Lutherans, they had a message for the entire nation. They organized and financed *The International Lutheran Hour,* and today support it at a cost of $1,425,000 a year.

The laymen, intensely upholding the sanctity of family life, have also been leaders in Lutheranism's ultra-modern attitude toward social service. They early adopted the foster-home method of rearing orphans, and the care of the aged in their own homes rather than in institutions. They hold that the family is the foundation of human existence and must be preserved, even for orphans and old people. Traditionally, Lutherans have been concerned with the welfare of the individual. They have 462 health and welfare agencies and institutions, staffed by more than 12,000 doctors, nurses and social workers.

Lutherans have also been more active than any other Protestant denomination in providing chaplains for hospitals, penitentiaries and private industries, and in establishing unusual facilities for the rehabilitation of the deaf and blind. The Missouri Synod alone has done more work among the deaf than all other Protestant bodies combined. It maintains seventy-seven churches for the deaf, which are served by forty-five full-time pastors. In these respects, Lutherans have made large contributions to American life.

During World War II, many Lutheran soldiers who served throughout the world returned home conscious of a religious isolation. They felt that Lutherans were perhaps too provincial and too conservative. In response to their insistence, the United Lutheran Church in 1948 ordered a study of Lutheran social attitudes. This work, completed in 1957 after nine years of inquiry by the Church's best scholars, drew a startling conclusion. It advised Lutherans that to be personal Good Samaritans was not enough; they must make their Church the conscience of society at large.

This is a new concept for Lutherans. It opens the doors for greater co-operation with other churches, with interchurch movements and with social-action agencies that, in the past, have been taboo in many synods. An enthusiastic Denver pastor of a United Lutheran Church congregation, after reading the new doctrine of social outreach, told his people, "We have waited three hundred years for this." He then proposed a resolution, at the annual meeting of the Rocky Mountain Synod, that Congress be petitioned not to reduce its foreign-aid program. Much to his surprise, this historic change from the nonpolitical tradition of Muhlenberg passed the conference with only a ripple of debate.

Thus American Lutheranism is in transition. It bristles with new members, new churches, new schools, new ideas with which to adorn an unchanging faith.

The next ten years will indeed be interesting. As one Lutheran authority put it, ". . . the Lutheran Church is in a state of ferment. . . . The situation is exceedingly fluid, new alignments are the order of the day, and when the present movement has run its course, it is almost certain that American Lutheranism will present a picture radically different from the present scene."

Lutherans agree that it will be different. But they shudder to think that it may be radical. To them, "radical" is a most objectionable word.

4

The Presbyterians

HISTORIANS GENERALLY AGREE that America is primarily the product of religious impacts. From the founding of Jamestown and Plymouth to the present day, religious influences have shaped —and continue to temper—most aspects of American life. The Presbyterians prove this historical point very well. They have contributed as much as any other denomination to the America we know today.

The Presbyterian hand is everywhere: in social crusades, public welfare, government, education and missions. Members consider all these as obligations of Christian citizenship. They will stand up and fight for any good cause, even when their position is unpopular.

"When our church is truly convinced of something," says Dr. Glenn W. Moore, secretary of the General Council of the United Presbyterian Church in the U.S.A., "it acts. The implications of our message must be faced in the practical life of persons and communities."

The Little Rock racial struggle is a good example of this. Within several days after the 1954 Supreme Court decision on school integration, the Southern Presbyterians passed a resolution urging compliance. The United Presbyterian Church, which has almost 300,000 Southerners in its nationwide membership, went even farther. When Governor Orval E. Faubus of Arkansas closed Little Rock's Central High School in 1958, two United Presbyterians issued from New York a statement on racial problems arguing that the use of "troops and tanks" to open the school would, "however unfortunate," be preferable to the continued denial of rights to Negro citizens and massive resistance to law.

In 1953, when the late Senator Joseph McCarthy was at his peak, the Presbyterians were among the first influential organized voices which dared to oppose his methods and the thinking he represented.

On the local level, political cleanup campaigns are often of Presbyterian inspiration. In Clarksburg, West Virginia, the Reverend Paul E. Francis helped organize the citizens to throw out an inefficient city administration, revise the city charter and revitalize the schools in 1954-55. For this achievement, the city won a *Look* 1957 All America City Award for self-improvement.

The Presbyterians also provide more of the leadership in interchurch and social agencies, from county councils of churches to national organizations, than any other faith, regardless of size. Such activities, considered extracurricular by most churches, are lifeblood to many Presbyterians.

Co-operative zeal is basic to Presbyterians. They feel compelled to work with other Protestants. Proud to be Presbyterians, they value the total number of world Christians, and most of them put the total cause first.

Thus they work hard for the National and World Councils of Churches, United Church Men, Church World Service, the Y.M.C.A., the American Bible Society and kindred bodies. For example, Dr. Eugene Carson Blake, Stated Clerk of the United Church, has been president of the National Council of Churches. In foreign-missionary fields, where they employ about two thousand missionaries, they often consolidate their efforts with those of other churches and throw their great resources behind governmental agencies and the United Nations in resettlement, refugee and child-welfare work. All over America, too, Presbyterians have led in the merger of congregations in several hundred communities into nondenominational Protestant churches.

A venerable quip says, "The Methodists shout, 'Fire, fire,' the Baptists cry, 'Water, water,' but the Presbyterians insist on 'Order, order.'" This organizational efficiency often causes them to gravitate to positions of power. Dwight D. Eisenhower is a Presbyterian, as was the late Secretary of State John Foster Dulles, along with three United States Supreme Court associate justices, eleven senators and forty-five representatives in Congress. President Eisenhower is the sixth Presbyterian to occupy the White House, following Buchanan, Jackson, Benjamin Harrison, Cleveland and Wilson. Four other Presidents worshiped with the Presbyterians while they were in Washington: Polk, Pierce, Lincoln and Grant.

The Church is so organized that laymen and clergy have equal voice. The name "Presbyterian" derives from the Greek word *presbyteros,* meaning "elder." In the first two centuries of Christianity, many churches were governed by elected representatives chosen from the elder and wiser members, who formed a "session" over which the minister presided. As handed down to modern times, the session rules the local congregation; several churches in the same vicinity are organized into a presbytery; all the presbyteries in a given area, usually a state, form a synod, and the presbyteries together comprise a general assembly. At every level, half the delegates must be laymen. Presbyterians believe in strong authority, but this power is never given to an individual, such as a bishop, but only to a group of elders. Ministers are often called "teaching elders," while laymen are termed "ruling elders." Thus Presbyterians are so called not from their theology, but from their type of organization.

The stress on education goes so deep that not even a Sunday-school teacher is accepted who has not passed a training course. Almost no important decision is taken without a survey to justify it.

In colonial America, almost all the Presbyterian clergy were graduates of European colleges. These learned ministers set up academies along with their churches, often to eke out their slim salaries by teaching. All over America, the academies expanded into great institutions of learning. Princeton, founded in 1746 as the College of New Jersey, was the first. The Presbyterians also joined with the Congregationalists on the frontier to open a number of schools, which were nicknamed "Presbygational" colleges. By the Civil War, the Presbyterians had 49 senior colleges spanning the country, even out to California and Oregon, while all other denominations together had only 131.

From Presbyterian schools have stemmed the state universities of Indiana, Tennessee, Delaware, Wisconsin, California, Georgia and Kentucky, and dozens of now-private institutions. Still affiliated with the various Presbyterian bodies are fifty-five colleges and eighteen theological seminaries.

The distinctive Presbyterian traits stem from the theology of John Calvin, the French religious reformer and a product of the sixteenth-century Reformation begun by Martin Luther. Calvin set up in Geneva, Switzerland, a model church government organized as are the modern Presbyterians. Doctrinally, Calvin believed that education and industry, public welfare and human rights must go hand in hand with religion. To Calvin, "man's chief end is to glorify God," who is a spirit with complete sovereignty over human affairs. The Church, being the executive agency of Christianity, must further God's will by social concern for all people. Calvin's movement was known as the Reformed Church. It produced the French Huguenots, the Dutch Reformed Church, the Church of Scotland, the Reformed Church of Hungary; in England, it evolved as Puritanism, which under Parliament and the Cromwells was for eleven years the state church.

It is commonly believed that American Presbyterians are descended from the Scottish Church. Actually, they include all the Reform elements from many nations. Presbyterianism reached the American colonies with the English Puritans, of whom there were two varieties. The Congregationalists insisted that the local congregation was the source of church authority, and settled all matters by majority vote. The Presbyterians emphasized world-wide Christianity and placed power in the hands of elders, elected by the congregation, and in the presbyteries.

Of the first thirty-three Puritan churches in Massachusetts, two were almost completely Presbyterian in organization. Cotton Mather stated that four thousand Presbyterians were in New England by 1640. There were enough Presbyterians in the Jamestown Colony by 1611 to form a church. But in New England, Congregationalism became the state church, and in Virginia, the Church of England was exclusive. As a result, the Presbyterians were largely expelled, or migrated voluntarily, to the middle colonies of New York, New Jersey, Pennsylvania, Maryland and Delaware.

Here they prospered. The first Presbyterian church in America with a continuous existence was founded in Jamaica, Long Island, in 1662. There were Presbyterians in New York City by 1678. The Presbyterians organized in Philadelphia in 1698; in Delaware, around the same year.

The Presbyterians had no unity until the coming of Francis Makemie. A Scotch-Irish missionary, Makemie was sent in 1683 to the Chesapeake Bay area by the presbytery of Laggan, in northern Ireland. On him is bestowed the title "Father of American Presbyterianism." After founding six churches, he led in the organization of the colonies' first presbytery in 1705 or 1706. This group included congregations in Maryland, Delaware and Pennsylvania, and soon afterward in New York.

From it were to grow the main arteries of United States Presbyterianism.

Makemie's work was completed just in time, for about 1705 began a seventy-year migration, mostly from the north of Ireland and Scotland, of a half-million settlers with Calvinist convictions.

Makemie's original presbytery had grown by 1717 into four presbyteries with three thousand members, and a synod was formed. This move induced many Congregational churches in New York and New Jersey to join, doubling the constituency. The attraction here was that the Presbyterian Synod disclaimed any tie to a foreign "mother church." Such forthright independence was popular politically. In 1729, the synod made the first formal statement by any American religious group advocating the separation of church and state by denying the power of magistrates to "persecute any for their religion."

The early Presbyterian churches were spartan. No hymns were allowed, only psalm singing. The local elders functioned as a court of morals, demanding public confession from members guilty of such sins as drunkenness, dancing, gambling, card playing, immodesty or night revels. At service, the sermons and prayers lasted for hours. Only those persons who had faithfully attended service were permitted to take communion, administered four times a year. To be sure no sinners gained admittance, each pastor had small coins cast from lead and stamped with his initials. These "communion tokens" were passed out in advance to be surrendered to the elders at the communion table.

The pastors received about a hundred British pounds a year in salary, plus manse and firewood and occasionally a clothing allowance. They augmented this in many ways. Since all were learned, they were much in demand as schoolmasters, tutors, bookkeepers and judges. They also were community leaders. When Indian raids killed eighty Presbyterians on the Pennsylvania frontier in 1754, the Reverend John (Fighting Pastor) Elder organized a band of rangers. Other ministers also led in the defense of the frontier during the French-Indian War.

By the Revolution, the Presbyterians numbered perhaps twenty thousand. In the middle colonies, the scene of heavy fighting, they were most numerous. Of fifty-five members of the Continental Congress who signed the Declaration of Independence, twelve were Presbyterians, not counting Benjamin Franklin, whose religious status is in doubt. They were rallied to the Revolution by, among others, John Witherspoon, president of the College of New Jersey (Princeton), who, in a volatile sermon on May 17, 1776, proclaimed the colonists' cause to be truly Calvinistic in its insistence on justice and liberty. So quick were Presbyterians to accept this cause that, by October, the presbytery in Hanover, Virginia, had publicly acclaimed the Declaration of Independence.

As a result of the Church's strong resistance, Presbyterian property was the target of British wrath. Sanctuaries and manses were burned. At Huntington, Long Island, British troops contemptuously built a blockhouse in the Presbyterian cemetery, and churches in New York City and New Brunswick, New Jersey, were used as cavalry stables. Entire congregations were scattered, never to re-form.

Preoccupation with war did not deter the Presbyterians from their spiritual obligations. Their missionary work among the Indians continued. When war stopped the importation of religious books, Robert Aitken, a Philadelphia elder fresh from a British military jail, published, in 1782, "the Aitken Bible," the first printed in English in America.

The end of the war found the Presbyterians weakened, many of their churches and schools destroyed, their boldest leadership killed in war or enticed into civil life. Furthermore, as settlers swept westward, the Presbyterians were bewildered by the illiteracy of the frontiersmen, and let them slip away to the Methodists and the Baptists. The Reverend David Rice, writing from Kentucky in 1783, expressed his despair as follows: "I could not think a church formed of such materials could properly be called a Church of Christ. With this I am distressed and made to cry, 'Where am I?' "

Thousands of frontier people, determined to remain Presbyterians, but scorning the rigid requirements of college training, organized the Cumberland Presbytery. By 1829, it had 170,000 members, chiefly in Ohio, Kentucky and farther south.

The main body of Presbyterianism held firmly to its standards, rebuilding slowly if not spectacularly. In 1812, Samuel J. Mills reported that there were only 49 Presbyterian and Congregational ministers in Ohio, one Presbyterian in Indiana and none at all in Illinois. But the breakdown of Congregational and Church of Eng-

land monopoly gave the Presbyterians wide gains in settled communities. The Londonderry Presbytery, an
independent body representing church members in New
England, joined the synod—now a general assembly—
in 1809. Large accessions were counted in Virginia and
the Carolinas. By 1830, the assembly had more than
173,000 worshipers, and by 1837, it was a truly national
denomination of 220,557, with an organization and
schools in all of the 26 states, and missionaries from
coast to coast.

The following years produced several splits and
schisms. Arguments between denominational-minded
elements, called the "old school," and the more inter-
denominational-minded, dubbed the "new school," divided the main branch into two arms in 1837. These
functioned separately until 1869, when they reunited
their 446,561 constituents into the Presbyterian Church
in the United States of America. Both the Old and New
School assemblies had lost their Southern members by
1861. The Southern Presbyterians consolidated, between
1861 and 1865, into what is now the Presbyterian
Church in the United States, better known as the
"Southern Presbyterians." This body, today numbering
873,071, remains independent, a regional denomination
operating in 16 Southern states plus Ohio, New Mexico
and Pennsylvania. Part of the Cumberland Presbytery
rejoined the Presbyterian Church in the U.S.A. in 1906,
but enough members declined the merger to preserve
the independent body, now numbering 86,000. In 1958,
another group, called the United Presbyterian Church of
North America, composed of conservative Scottish

groups, which had flourished since 1774, merged its 311,025 members with the Presbyterian Church in the U.S.A. to form a national denomination of 3,102,572 under the name United Presbyterian Church in the U.S.A. The Southerners and other independents contributed to a total Presbyterian membership in 1958 of about 4,134,502, making the Presbyterians the fourth largest Protestant group in America.

Generally speaking, Presbyterians are upper-middle class; however there is a rapidly increasing constituency among the so-called underprivileged: the Spanish-speaking, the Indians, the Negroes, the slum dwellers. A survey of families subscribing to *Presbyterian Life* in 1958 showed that 72 per cent of the women were housewives with no other employment. Of the men, 29 per cent were in learned professions, 12.2 per cent were business executives, 13 per cent skilled craftsmen, only 3.8 per cent farmers. More than half (54.2) of the men and 38.9 of the women had attended college. The average family income was $6,165, and 83.5 per cent of the surveyed families owned their own homes.

The Presbyterians were the first United States denomination to establish a national agency to promote domestic missions. Makemie's little synod had grown by 1789 into a general assembly, which created, in 1802, a Standing Committee of Missions. This committee published, in 1803, a sermon by Henry Kollock of Elizabethtown, New Jersey, entitled "Christ Must Increase," which stated, seventy-five years ahead of the so-called "social gospel," that Christians had a social responsibility to the pioneer, Negro and Indian.

Work among the Indians began in Colonial times, when Azariah Horton established a mission on Long Island in 1742. For three years, from 1744 to 1747, David Brainerd, though dying of tuberculosis, traveled the Alleghenies ministering to the Delaware Indians. His journal, edited by the New England intellectual Jonathan Edwards, was published posthumously. Considered an epic, it inspired Presbyterians to Indian missionary work with such fervor that the denomination is to this day a leader in the field. Samuel Worcester, around 1840, translated the Bible into Cherokee, and Dr. Thomas S. Williamson gave the Bible to the Dakotas. Henry Rowe Schoolcraft learned Chippewa customs so thoroughly that his book *Algic Researches* was used by Longfellow as the basis for *Hiawatha*. In 1832, Schoolcraft explored the sources of the Mississippi River, and called attention to the vast iron-ore deposits in Minnesota's Mesabi Range.

The most spectacular Presbyterian domestic missionaries were Dr. Marcus and Narcissa Whitman and Henry and Eliza Spalding, who in 1836 followed the Oregon Trail—the first time that women and wagons had gone west overland—and set up missions among the Cayuse and Nez Percé Indians in Oregon Territory. In 1842, Whitman set out alone for the East on horseback through a bitter winter, surviving blizzards and crossing icy rivers. He returned with a thousand settlers, giving the United States a stronger position in the Oregon dispute with Britain.

In Alaska, Presbyterians maintain among the Eskimos the northernmost Protestant mission on the

American continent, a six-hundred-mile stretch of coast-
line within the Arctic Circle. In Alaska's recent successful fight for statehood, one of the leaders was a
Presbyterian minister, the Reverend R. Rolland Arm-
strong, a member of the Constitutional Convention.

The denomination's unflagging concern for the Indians compels the Church today to maintain missions,
schools and hospitals on reservations in 16 states. But
that is only one aspect of domestic missionary achievement. The two largest bodies of United States Presbyterians both have extensive ministries among migrant
workers and minority groups. There is a Japanese-
language church in Chicago, a Chinese congregation in
New Orleans, an Italian settlement in Kansas City, a
Yiddish mission for the Jews in Baltimore. There are
roundups for cowboys in the Southwestern states. There
are "Sunday-school missionaries" in remote Western
areas who in 1957 traveled a total of 1,098,881 miles.
In Idaho, the Reverend J. H. Howell covers his 25,000-
square-mile parish by airplane, visiting the sick, starting
church schools and serving the spiritual needs of families
living 40 to 50 miles apart. The tremendous effort within United States borders involved the United Presbyterians and the Southern branch in 3,567 projects involving 3,036 missionaries during 1958.

In social welfare, the Presbyterians are equally energetic. As early as 1910, the denomination was active in
settlement work, the crusade against child labor, the
movements for better working conditions, slum clearance, arbitration of labor-management disputes and

similar causes. Today, both major Presbyterian general assemblies maintain trouble shooters who move into areas of tension and help local churches solve social problems. In 1958, these staffs were involved in the racial problem in the South and in the blighted areas of big cities. The Presbyterians no longer abandon downtown churches when the members have moved to the suburbs. They rebuild them when possible for the underprivileged who move into the areas. Continuing studies of social maladjustments give the Church a good idea of what should be done. Presbyterians have long since, for example, relaxed early Puritanical attitudes on smoking, dancing and other social customs.

At the moment, Presbyterian scholars are investigating such divergent fields as automation, United States foreign policy, family planning (Presbyterians do not disapprove of planned parenthood), delinquency, the new suburbs, the new leisure. The United Presbyterian Church called on all members to end segregation in residential housing.

A study by the Southern Church showed that the present generation of Negroes, with better education and higher earning power, were often no longer content with the emotional type of religion generally associated with the race. Negro churches stressing dignity and scholarship have been established in twenty-four key Southern cities. Southern Presbyterian Negro membership doubled between 1953 and 1958.

In addition, Presbyterians support 133 community centers and neighborhood houses, 59 hospitals and clinics, 105 institutional chaplains, 14 children's homes and 69 homes for the aged.

Such activities require money, and the Presbyterians give it. In 1957, members of what is now the United Presbyterian Church in U. S. A. contributed $233,393,-239, or $76.75 per member. The Southerners did even better per capita, leading all major denominations with $92.41, a total of $78,431,401.

How do Presbyterians do it? By emphasizing the obligation of every member to Christ. They maintain that man needs to give back to God, for the good of his own soul, at least some part of what God has given the individual. In what is now the United Church, giving has increased 145 per cent in the past 10 years.

In 1948, a new study program was inaugurated, de-emphasizing the ivory tower and traditional concepts of teaching religion. Substituted was an emphasis on faith applied to everyday life. It ties family, school, church and prayer into an integrated whole, related at every step to personal experience. The program is bolstered by lavish visual aids, manuals for home use, the family magazine *Presbyterian Life* and hundreds of books. So attractive is the new literature that seventy-five titles published by The Westminster Press for church use have been chosen by religious book clubs for national distribution.

The result of all this is a new accent on spiritual life which deeply commits the entire family, a religious upsurge which the Church has not achieved in a generation. No longer is church life largely motivated by women, who, in turn, insist on the participation of the children. Even the laymen, who by and large had begun to consider churchgoing a community activity on a par with Rotary Clubs or a social identification they could not afford to be without, have been swept into spiritual participation in the Church and personal prayer life. Today, one out of every four Presbyterian Sunday-school teachers is a man—usually a father—and 750,000 Presbyterian men work for Christ through the denomination's men's clubs.

Because the Church offers members the chance to work for a living faith with meaning for a modern world, the Presbyterians in the past decade have experienced the greatest growth in their history. The Southerners have enrolled 210,868 new members in the past 10 years, a gain of 32.9 per cent. Churches in the United Presbyterian Church gained 23 per cent in a like period. The Presbyterians are on the move everywhere: in the slums, the Indian reservations, the suburbs, the countryside. They are organizing four new churches a week. All this is carefully planned. In 1947, for example, the Reverend Robert H. Meneilly was sent by the United Presbyterian Board of American Missions to build a congregation from an empty lot in Prairie Village, Kansas. A manse and sanctuary were erected before charter members were received. Ten years later, the church had 3,400 members.

The Presbyterians have trailer churches, drive-in churches, migrant churches, Spanish-settlement churches, warehouse churches and congregations in private homes. The Southerners recently recommended the purchase of

seventy-one farm-land locations which their surveys indicate will be the heart of suburbs within a few years,
and they are now searching for young men to educate
as clergymen to fill these as-yet-nonexistent pulpits.

The Presbyterians rejoice in their dynamic growth.
But, true to tradition, they are aware of the influx into
many churches of "Sunday shoppers," who leave any
congregation which makes demands on them. The
Presbyterians will take these folk, all right; but then, in
Presbyterian fashion, will set out to educate them into
the obligations of being a Christian.

To be a Presbyterian, you must believe devoutly that
God has first place in your life. And you must work
hard in the Church and in the community, giving lavishly
of both your money and your talents. Otherwise, you
will feel very uncomfortable, because that's what
Presbyterians are like.

5

The Congregationalists

MANY OF THE CUSTOMS and beliefs that sum up "The American Way of Life" are the product of the New England religious experiment known as the Congregational Way. For this tradition, if for nothing else, every living American is in debt to the first settlers of Massachusetts.

The Pilgrims and Puritans gave us not only Congregationalism, but also Thanksgiving, the town meeting, our first university, our first coeducational college, public schools and Mother Goose. They started the Revolution (the Minute Men at Lexington and Concord were Congregationalists almost to a man). They brought the civil liberties of England's Magna Carta to the American continent. They helped develop in America the system of free enterprise.

More intangibly, the Puritans bestowed upon the American spirit a dogged reliance on Providence, a faith in our ability to win over any odds, a restlessness and inability to settle down, a humility before God and, at the same time, a vaulting egoism that refuses to admit any human authority as our master. These characteristics are stamped on the American personality; they were impressed there by the Puritans.

In recent years, many efforts have been made to

debunk the Puritans. The objective has been to minimize our cultural heritage and thus open the door to opposing philosophies. Yet so deeply rooted is Puritanism that it still defends America against scores of ideologies by the strength of its tradition alone.

Modern Congregationalism has reached out so far from its New England provincialism that today the Congregational churches are in process of becoming part of a larger body known as the United Church of Christ. But because of the tenacity with which Congregationalists uphold the authority of the local church to govern its own affairs, some of the 5,506 local fellowships, which today total 1,401,565 members, probably will continue to be known as Congregational Christian churches.

Paradoxically, Congregationalism also has a history of reactionary traditions. The stubbornness with which the colonial Puritans insisted that only members of their church could be citizens was a prime factor in the demand of the Baptists and others that separation of church and state should be guaranteed in the United States Constitution. The blue laws, which made the adjective "puritanical" represent strict morality and strait-laced orthodoxy, helped bring such an intellectual revolt that modern Congregationalism is quite liberal.

The rigidity with which the Congregational churches imposed their austere Calvinism was one reason why many thousands of New Englanders migrated to the West after the Revolutionary War. Thus Congregational ethics and theology indirectly influenced the constitution and folkways of every new state from Ohio to California. Many of the migrant pioneers from New England joined other denominations. Their influence nailed to all of Protestantism the Puritans' concern for human welfare and their reliance on the Bible as the primary source of man's inspiration. Wherever Puritan descendants have resettled, they have taken New England with them and transplanted its ethos in new soil.

Now another paradox is transforming the Congregationalists. They have become some of the most aggressive Protestant organizers in the cities of America. This is strange, since they had long accepted the prevailing Protestant concept that Christianity thrives only when it is nurtured by small-town, middle-class respectability. For three centuries, American Protestants by and large have regarded the city as primarily evil, unsuited to the development of Christian life. They have attempted to impose village morals and attitudes on city residents, stifling the development of a characteristically urban culture. In the words of Dr. Truman B. Douglass, executive vice-president of the Congregational Christian Board of Home Missions, Protestantism "disparages the intensity of the metropolitan experience as if [it] were morally inferior to the prosaic dead-level dullness of American life in the typical town or village."

Dr. Douglass pointed the denomination toward a bold new course in 1958 when he said, "If the church is to serve the city, it must first learn to love the city." The Congregationalists, therefore, have moved with great vigor among the slums and skyscrapers. Typical of their work is the career of the Reverend J. Archie Hargraves. In 1948, he helped to establish the East Harlem Protestant Parish in New York. This today is a large-scale interdenominational effort, serving inter-racial areas in the heart of slums by the use of store-front chapels, the capable direction of boys' and girls' clubs, and broad community service.

Hargraves then moved on to the West Side Christian Parish in Chicago, where in 1951 he opened a mission in an empty store. This work has grown into an organization of eleven ministers and seven social centers. In 1956, he became pastor of the Nazarene Congregational Church in Brooklyn, New York. Here was a parish described by the Board of Home Missions as possessing "almost every problem that plagues city churches throughout the country." More than 62,000 persons live within a mile of the church. Hargraves saw this area as one having a vast potential, with thousands of families who wanted Christ and a better life for themselves, but had no idea how to organize for their common benefit.

With the aid of the denomination, Hargraves has created a pilot project in Brooklyn. It is developing techniques for answering the Christian needs of city dwellers. Hargraves has set up "halfway houses" in vacant stores, to draw area residents off the streets. Block workers mingle with the neighborhood youth, especially with the "left-out" teen-agers who have been rejected by their age group. An evangelist covers the crowded tenements, much as an old-time politician would cover his ward or precinct. A community co-ordinator inspires civic organizations to prosecute gouging landlords and to build a better neighborhood together. The Congregational Home Mission Board considers the

Nazarene experiment "one of the most significant under-
takings in Protestantism."

Throughout America, the Congregationalists, and
the Evangelical and Reformed Church with which the
Congregationalists are now uniting, have met the challenge of the city head-on. Chicago is a good example
of the results.

At the Warren Avenue Congregational Church,
which fifty years ago had an upper-class congregation,
the ministers serve a fluid tenement population of mixed
races. A unique feature is two simultaneous Sunday-
morning sermons, one in English, the other in Spanish.
The pastors also keep regular office hours, like doctors,
for personal counseling.

At the Wellington Avenue Congregational Church
on Chicago's Near North Side, the problem involves
ministering to a community that includes both luxury
apartments and slums. Park Manor Church, in turn,
serves prosperous Negroes, 1,100 of whom have joined
the congregation in the past six years. Christ Congregational Church's Japanese-born pastor attracts Japanese-
Americans from all over the city. South Congregational
Church, so stripped by the flight of its members to the
suburbs that in 1958 it lost its edifice through bank-
ruptcy, is now reorganizing in the new housing developments. These are typical of the 79 Congregational and
Evangelical and Reformed churches in inner Chicago
that the denomination has refused to abandon.

So thoroughly have Congregationalists attacked the
city and its problems that they even maintain a special

ministry to the beatniks in San Francisco. Pierre Delattre, pastor of the Bread and Wine Mission, as it is
called, operates from a North Beach store. He doesn't
strive for conversions; instead, he and his "parishioners"
usually end up "preaching to one another." One of
Delattre's problems involves the college students who
arrive in San Francisco each summer to emulate the
much-publicized "beat" colony. Many of his contacts
are made by visits to psychiatric clinics and neighborhood
taverns.

All this excitement has not in the least disturbed the
traditional "village-green" fellowships of New England
and elsewhere. Under Congregational policy, each congregation is a self-contained unit. It establishes its own
constitution and creed and is free to conduct its own
affairs within the denomination. This independence is,
in sum, the essence of the Congregational spirit. The
founders of the denomination were vehement dissenters
against many observances of their own time. They were
revolutionaries with definite ideas about the right of
each individual to work out his spiritual destiny, under
Christ, in his own way.

The Pilgrims held their first service on the soil of
America on January 21, 1621, less than six weeks after
they landed at Plymouth. By the time the Puritans arrived from England and settled in Salem, in 1628, the
Plymouth community numbered three hundred. The
Pilgrims had lived twelve years in Holland, but they
differed scarcely at all from the Puritans, who were so
called from their zeal to purify the Anglican Church of
all Roman Catholic influences not removed by the

Reformation. Both groups were religious radicals. They protested against the social order, as well as against many customs of the established church. They were determined to create their own idea of a religious state and to apply their Calvinism to everyday life, whether the majority agreed with them or not. Thus they were nuisances, and English authorities were not sorry to see them leave.

They called their church Congregational because of its system of rule, which developed from necessity. For nine years, the Pilgrims had no ordained preacher among them. Thus they were compelled to set up a religious community governed by majority vote of the laymen. As a result, civil marriage was recognized from the first wedding, there were no church funerals, and the elders quickly imposed their will on all the people. When ordained clergy finally arrived, they were elected to their pastorates.

Written agreements were made among the colonists to provide for civil government. The first, the Mayflower Compact, sustained the Plymouth government until the colony merged with Massachusetts seventy-one years later. Church and state became inseparable in 1631, when the Puritans agreed that only members of their religious fellowship could be voting citizens. (This by no means implied that all the voters were devout.) Such rigid requirements were set up that in 1640, when the Massachusetts Bay Colony numbered fifteen thousand, only about three thousand were even considered to be Christians; hence, four out of five had no political citizenship and no vote. Yet, at first, everyone was required to attend church, and everyone was taxed for its support. The town meeting, which made civil laws, was merely an extension of the church meeting, since the same persons voted in each.

By 1640, Massachusetts had thirty-three towns. All of them were ruled by the members of the Congregational churches. Newcomers were required to review their lives publicly and to prove that they were "saints." If the congregation rejected them, they were considered damned; those accepted into membership were the elect of God.

The churches solidified into a denomination when their representatives, called into a synod meeting by the General Court of Massachusetts, adopted the Cambridge Platform in 1648. The individual freedom of each congregation was guaranteed, and members were joined by a covenant they all agreed to obey. The pastors formed a closer association in 1690, when a ministerial organization was founded in the Boston area.

The tight church grip on the populace failed to survive for very long. In 1689, the British Parliament passed an Act of Toleration, which forced all the colonies to permit freedom of worship. But the state church continued in New Hampshire and Connecticut until well after the Revolution, and in die-hard Massachusetts until 1834.

As early as 1662, many descendants of the original settlers, failing to pass the stern church-membership requirements, forced adoption of a "Half-Way Covenant."

This entitled their children to baptism and the right to vote in town elections, but not to full church membership or communion unless they met the church's rigid requirements. The result was a wave of liberalism and antireligiousness. By 1700, Puritanism as a daily influence and a political dictatorship had ended. Laymen succeeded the churchmen in leadership, and the pulpit lost much of its thunder. The reaction continued for many years. In 1825, when the American Unitarian Association was formed, the Congregationalists lost to it 125 New England churches, including the original one at Plymouth, all but two fellowships in Boston and 20 of the first 25 Congregational gatherings in the New World.

Meanwhile, the Connecticut churches had developed along a slightly different path. Thomas Hooker, pastor at what is now Cambridge, Massachusetts, migrated with his flock to the vicinity of Hartford in 1636, and two years later broke away from the domination of the Massachusetts church. Hooker's constitution gave suffrage to most males, whether they were church members or not.

Long before the New England preachers had lost their influence, they were laying the groundwork for the later Revolution. They all preached "election sermons"; they were the chief orators at political rallies. Before the day of newspapers, the ministers were the editorial pages of the colony. Dr. Jonathan Mayhew of Boston preached that the colonists had a sacred duty to resist tyranny. Thomas Hooker at Hartford insisted that no political authority was valid unless the voters consented to it. He also advocated a written political constitution, in contrast to the unwritten code of England, so that its provisions would be clear to everyone. John Wise of Ipswich popularized the idea of "No taxation without representation," and is often called the "father" of the Revolution.

After passage of the Stamp Act in 1765, Congregational ministers argued that liberty had become a holy cause. When the war broke out, dozens of preachers raised military units and accompanied them into battle.

Due to this activity, and to the collapse of many Anglican communions, Congregationalism was the most influential religious voice in America at the close of the Revolution, but the denomination failed to hold its position. The Connecticut churches made an agreement with the Presbyterians for joint work in the West, and most of the Yankee frontiersmen who joined this "Presbygational" union became Presbyterians within a half century. The unchurched affiliated largely with the Methodists and Baptists. This was a setback for Congregationalism. Having no hierarchy or strong centrality, the Puritan descendants had no organization for following the population as it swept across the continent.

However, the Congregationalists made many isolated gains. The first Protestant church in the Northwest Territory was theirs, founded at Marietta, Ohio, in 1796. By 1850, there were 131 Congregational churches in Ohio, despite heavy defections to the Presbyterians. The first Protestant church in California was Congregationalist; United States Navy chaplain Walter Colton formed it at Monterey shortly after the territory was taken from Mexico in 1846. Seven out of ten Congregationalists lived in New England in 1860; but by 1890, more than half of the churches and members were located outside that area. Today, the United Church of Christ is eighth in size among United States Protestant bodies, with churches in every state.

The story of Congregationalism includes the names of many of the nation's great reformers and theologians. The colonial era produced John Cotton, John Davenport, Thomas Hooker and Cotton Mather, all among the foremost men of their day. Later, Jonathan Edwards led a phenomenal New England revival. In the nineteenth century, Dwight L. Moody helped shake Congregationalism loose from conservatism, and Francis E. Clark led the founding of the Society of Christian Endeavor. The slavery issue was almost a Congregational monopoly for some years. Henry Ward Beecher in Brooklyn and Leonard Bacon in New Haven inflamed the entire upper Eastern Seaboard against the South. Bacon's treatise *Slavery Discussed* deeply influenced Abraham Lincoln. Lyman Beecher of Cincinnati, who became a Presbyterian, was one of the organizers of the Anti-Slavery Society.

During the nineteenth century, the Congregational churches were leaders in the establishment of the social-gospel movement. Such men as Lyman Abbott, Amory Bradford and Washington Gladden championed the rights of labor and fought for social services. They taught that the Gospel applied to social as well as individual relations. Today, this work is carried on by the

Council for Social Action, which in recent years has supported such controversial causes as complete racial integration, extensive foreign aid and even the recognition of Red China.

An enlightened membership requires education. Harvard, established by the Puritans in 1636, was the first college in America. Yale was established in 1701, followed by Dartmouth, Williams and Amherst. Today, there are forty-seven colleges and universities with Congregational roots. Oberlin in Ohio was the first college in the world to admit women, in 1833. Oberlin was joined by the all-women colleges of Mount Holyoke, Smith and Wellesley, which were given financial support by Congregationalists. The first public school in America, supported by direct taxation, was started in 1639 by the Congregationalists at Dorchester, Massachusetts.

Significant leaders in Negro education, the Congregationalists were the first to open their doors to Negro college students (at Oberlin in 1835). At one time, the denomination had more than six hundred Negro schools, many of which today are outstanding state or independent institutions. In the South, six Congregational colleges serve Negroes.

From earliest times, the Congregationalists recognized the power of the printed word, and utilized it. They set up the first printing press in the colonies, and on it in 1640 printed the first book published in the colonies, *The Bay Psalm Book*.

The Congregationalists, too, have the oldest and most romantic missionary history of any American Protestant group. In 1641, Thomas Mayhew started preaching to the Indians on Martha's Vineyard. In 1646, the Reverend John Eliot began his work among the Indians around Newton, Massachusetts. He organized 14 Christian villages, which at their height included 1,100 souls. He also translated the Bible into Algonquin. This was the first Bible printed in the colonies.

The Congregationalists launched the first foreign-missionary movement in America. This organization arose from a discussion by five students at Williams College in 1806. The occasion is now famous as "The Haystack Prayer Meeting." The quintet, out for a walk, took refuge from a thundershower under a farmer's hay-stack. There, they agreed to spread the Gospel in foreign lands. Since the denomination had no organization to sponsor them, one had to be formed. Thus began what now is called the American Board of Commissioners for Foreign Missions. It soon became a joint effort with the Presbyterians and two Reformed groups, but the others ultimately withdrew. Ironically, the first missionary, Adoniram Judson, switched to the Baptists while en route to India. Undismayed, the Congregationalists proceeded to form a world-wide missionary enterprise.

Wherever they went, they took the school and the printing press with them. Hiram Bingham, for example, printed the first books and the first newspaper in Hawaii. By 1850, the far-flung missions of the American Board were publishing and teaching in 30 languages. The educational endeavor had great impact. At the United Nations organizational meeting in 1945, 29 Middle Eastern delegates were graduates of the American University, founded in Beirut, Lebanon, by the Congregationalists. The American Board maintains 760 schools and colleges abroad. The work of Dr. Frank C. Laubach, an American Board missionary, has achieved world renown. His technique of "each one teach one" is credited with freeing countless millions from illiteracy.

From the beginning, the missionary emphasis was on Christianity, not on denominationalism. Dr. Arthur Smith persuaded President Theodore Roosevelt to use Boxer Rebellion indemnities to finance the education of Chinese youth. Corinna Shattuck taught the art of linen making to thousands of widows and orphans in Asia Minor. The Congregational missions have attacked poverty, the subjugation of women, polygamy and caste as well as paganism. Today, more than half of the Board's 12,500 personnel are concerned with education, since the native fellowships have long since produced their own clergy and administrators. Overseas workers are no longer considered missionaries, but rather fraternal workers in the churches they serve.

In medical missions, the American Board also pioneered. Dr. John Scudder, the first medical missionary of modern times, was sent to India in 1819. Today, the Board has seventy-three hospitals in fourteen countries. Typical is a clinic and leper hospital at Kilanjunai in South India, conducted by Dr. Edward C. Riggs. He teaches classes in public health, gives inoculations, combats malnutrition and disseminates birth-control information. At Mount Salinda Hospital in Rhodesia, prenatal care and delivery cost a native mother $1.50; a clinic visit is 36¢, an appendectomy, $2.80.

The missionary and social-welfare preoccupations of Congregationalism encouraged closer co-operation among the individual congregations. The first state conference was established in Maine in 1826. A national association was cemented in 1871, with the founding of the National Council of Congregational Churches. In 1892, the fellowship was joined by a Congregational Methodist group, and in 1923 by the Evangelical Protestants and 250 German Congregational churches. In 1931, the Congregational churches united with the General Convention of the Christian Church to form the Congregational Christian Churches.

Then, in 1957, the denomination's General Council united with the Evangelical and Reformed Church to create a new denomination, the United Church of Christ. Since the Evangelical and Reformed communion is mostly German in racial origin and has a modified Presbyterian type of organization, the merger with the English-tradition Congregationalists is unique in American Protestant history. It is the first United States union of two fellowships of unlike traditions and differing forms of government.

Not all of the Congregationalists, however, have accepted this latest union—nor have they been asked to do so, since no constitution has yet been adopted. A resistant group, the National Association of Congregational Churches, has been formed; it mustered seventy-two congregations at a convention in 1959. A Central Association of Congregational Churches has been created for congregations which oppose the merger. Another small faction has organized as the League to Uphold Congregational Principles. To date, these movements have not had a serious impact upon the union.

If any single congregation typifies Congregationalism as a whole, it is perhaps Old South Church in Boston. This is one of the most famous churches in America, founded only forty-nine years after the arrival of the Mayflower. It was the only colonial Boston fellowship that remained true to Congregationalism in the defection to Unitarianism. Its pre-Revolutionary War edifice on Washington Street is now a public museum (the congregation moved in 1875 to Copley Square). The old building was the largest auditorium in Boston for more than a century, and thus became a center for patriotic meetings.

The Old South congregation first showed its fighting spirit when Sir Edmund Andros, sent as British governor to New England in 1686, declared the Puritan constitution invalid, took over the government and seized Old South for Anglican worship. The church's pastor, the Reverend Samuel Willard, led a militant opposition to Andros. For this action these men could have lost their heads. But when word came that King James II had been dethroned, Andros was kicked out, in 1689.

A church member, Judge Samuel Sewall, presided at some of the infamous witch trials at Salem. But he regretted condemning the victims to death, and wrote out a statement of error, which was read in Old South while the judge stood before the congregation, his head bowed in contrition. Sewall was also the author of *The Selling of Joseph,* the first antislavery tract in America.

Old South fostered many great persons and events. A colonial member, Elizabeth Vergoose, is said to have had the Mother Goose nursery rhymes published. During the French and Indian War, when the French sent a fleet to sack Boston, the Reverend Thomas Prince called a prayer meeting. While he prayed, a wind scattered the fleet.

As the Revolution approached, Old South was one of the centers of resistance to the British. Samuel Adams, a foremost revolutionary and an originator of the Continental Congress, used the church as a stage for incendiary speeches. His oration protesting the Boston Massacre was instrumental in forcing the British troops to evacuate the city. The men of the Boston Tea Party made Old South their rendezvous. William Dawes of Old South rode, as did Paul Revere, to warn Lexington and Concord of the first British attack.

The patriotic tradition continued into the Civil War. The Boston mass meeting that followed the firing on Fort Sumter was held in Old South. The edifice became a recruiting depot, where the Forty-Third Massachusetts Regiment was formed, with the church's minister, the Reverend J. M. Manning, as its chaplain. When Lee surrendered, the city's thanksgiving service was held in Old South.

Today, the church has all the problems common to the denomination. It is no longer in a village-green environment. Its influential parishioners have moved to the suburbs, leaving Old South to serve a checkered community of transients, slum dwellers and people living in deluxe apartments, plus a few old families who travel as far as thirty-five miles to church. Fully a third of the weekly congregation of nine hundred is made up of students from dozens of nearby colleges and schools. The church has twelve hundred members, but fifteen hundred others call Old South their spiritual home and draw on it for sustenance. Three clergy head a staff of twenty, which includes a social worker and two counselors expert in family life. Old South's church school, the largest in downtown Boston, is entirely staffed by paid professional teachers. Every year, on Thanksgiving Day, members return to their historic museum home on Washington Street for a memorial service.

Today, Old South lives on in the Puritan tradition. Its senior minister, Dr. Frederick M. Meek, on the occasion of the arrival of *Mayflower II* in 1957, epitomized this heritage:

"It is not enough to gather in celebration if we have no concern to be the kind of people the Pilgrims were, and if we ourselves are not moved by their example to be Pilgrims in our own time. . . . Our way of life is freedom to act as responsible citizens, sharing in the common civic and economic life of community and nation, so that what we as individuals choose to do could be adopted by all others, with harmful results to no one. It is the freedom of men who are brethren because God is their father."

Every Congregationalist, past and present, would endorse that.

6

The Roman Catholics

T HE ROMAN CATHOLIC CHURCH in the United States is three times the size of any other religious body in the country. It is vast, with 34,386,351 registered members in 16,260 parishes. It is complex, with 90 orders of priests and brothers and 276 orders of nuns, and of such diversity that sermons are delivered in more than 10 languages. It is the richest jewel in the world-wide Church, counting its income in billions of dollars and its property in tens of billions. Its members send more money to the Vatican for support of the Church around the world than do the Catholics in any other country. It spends a billion dollars a year on its United States educational system alone, and almost as much in charity through a network of 1,661 hospitals and homes. The administration of this tremendous structure is a larger undertaking than the management of General Motors and the American Telephone and Telegraph Company combined. The executive echelon, composed of four cardinals, 33 archbishops and 176 bishops, is typically American in that not one of these men is the son of a college graduate.

For all its size and wealth, its stupendous historical, religious, charitable and educational accomplishments, the Roman Catholic Church remains a subject of controversy and criticism. Its ultimate ends are looked upon with suspicion and fear, particularly when concepts of freedom are related to its action. Both spiritually and socially, the Catholic Church stands aloof, almost withdrawn, behind a wall it was forced to rear against anti-Catholic prejudice.

Recently, a distinguished jurist, William J. Brennan, Jr., on appointment to the United States Supreme Court, was required by a congressional committee to swear on oath that his Catholicism did not conflict with his Americanism. Ingrained in non-Catholic minds is the belief that eventually, given the chance, the Catholic Church will take over the country and suppress every religion and freedom except its own. That fear has been, and remains, the great obstruction that American Catholics have not been able to detour on the road to full acceptance.

From the creation of this nation, the Catholic Church has been one of the whipping boys of American life. There have been dormant periods in the antagonism toward Catholics in America, but there has never been peace. The country was settled at the height of Europe's religious wars. Catholics gained a toehold in the New World only after bitter opposition.

Catholic Maryland was the first colony to grant religious freedom, in 1649, in what is now the United States. But in 1691, William and Mary, then on the English throne, made Maryland a royal colony, and the Church of England became the state religion. Catholicism was suppressed. In 1704, the first Catholic church in Maryland, Saint Mary's Chapel, which was built in

1634, was locked and never used again. Worship was thereafter continued in private homes. Not many Catholics were involved. The Maryland census of 1708 tallied only 2,974 Catholics out of a population of 33,833.

The few Catholics who migrated to America during the next 70 years found refuge chiefly in William Penn's Quaker colony of Pennsylvania. There, Catholicism had been established feebly in 1681. As late as 1757, there were only 1,365 adult Catholics in Pennsylvania, and only a few dozen in New Jersey. By the end of the Revolution, American Catholics numbered perhaps 23,-000, of whom half were in Maryland, 7,000 in Pennsylvania, a few hundred at Vincennes in Indiana, the remainder scattered and without permanent priests or churches.

The dominance of Protestants in New England caused firm suppression of Catholic worship there until after the Revolutionary War. Cotton Mather, the clergyman and author, wrote that not one professing Catholic could be found in all New England in 1640, and the rumor of a Catholic Mass in a home in Boston proved to be false. Except for a few French Canadians settled in northern Maine, the first recorded Catholic migrants to New England were a hundred Ulster families who reached New Hampshire by 1719. Massachusetts, which was to be inundated by the Irish in the next hundred years, did not see public Catholic worship until 1788. Rhode Island, often believed to be an early Catholic refuge, had a resident priest in 1820 but did not have a Catholic church until 1829. Indeed, Catholicism was vigorously discouraged during the entire colonial period throughout New England.

So great was the colonial anti-Catholic spirit that, from 1691 until after the Revolution, no colony permitted legal, public Catholic worship or allowed any Catholic to hold public office. Despite this, the few Catholics in the colonies made notable contributions to the rebellion. A Catholic signed the Declaration of Independence, and two signed the Constitution. Thomas FitzSimons was General Washington's secretary, and John Barry was commander of the American Navy. Charles Carroll was so patriotic that he signed the Declaration of Independence with his address as well as his name, lest there be any doubt as to his identity; he, the richest man in the colonies, had the most to lose.

In the West, the American back door was guarded against the British at Detroit by Father Pierre Gibault, a missionary who persuaded Catholic settlers in Indiana territory to join the Revolution. Two of the most distinguished Revolutionary heroes were Catholics: Casimir Pulaski, cavalry leader, who died in battle, and Thaddeus Kosciusko, a hero of Saratoga.

The Catholics won freedom of worship in the Revolution, but not social acceptance. They might have achieved equal status, except for the Irish immigration shortly after the war, which revived and accentuated the traditional anti-Catholic spirit. Before Catholic prestige could be established, the potato blight struck Ireland, followed by the great famine of 1845-49. In 30 years, 1,041,000 Irish Catholics migrated to America. They were mainly illiterate, poor, unskilled. They possessed a fierce love for their religion and a passionate hatred for Protestantism, fired by centuries of English oppression. In many ways, they were distinct from Catholics of other countries. Their piety was severe, almost dour, their sexual mores were puritanical, and their attitude toward their priests was deeply reverential.

They settled in Eastern ports and immediately became a social problem. For the first time in America, pauperism required public relief. The national bill in 1837 was $4,000,000, and that of New York City alone, $279,000, the beneficiaries being chiefly Irish.

If the Irish, like the Jews, tended to be exclusive, prejudice made this withdrawal necessary for their very survival. To protect themselves against outbreaks in which their homes were burned, against job and religious discrimination, the Irish clanned together in the biggest cities, in tight, isolated areas usually labeled "shanty towns."

By 1830, an avowed anti-Irish-Catholic political party had been organized. Many outrages occurred, including the burning of a convent in Charlestown, Massachusetts, in 1834. The self-styled "Native Americans" who fostered this prejudice gave way later to an even more aggressive secret society. It was called the "Know Nothings" because, when asked about themselves, members replied, "I know nothing." By now, German immigration had begun. The Germans, being skilled and thrifty, took over many jobs and bought large areas of farm land, built parochial schools and preserved their language and customs. Here was a threat to job security and Americanism from another direction, while Irish immigration was still at its peak.

In 1844, a three-day riot between Catholics and Protestants occurred in Philadelphia, during which thirteen persons were killed and forty-two wounded, two Catholic churches and a seminary were burned, and seven-score Irish homes were destroyed. In the following years, such riots became commonplace. An Italian prelate, Archbishop Bedini, visiting the United States from Rome in 1853, was stoned and almost hanged in Cincinnati. The following year, in Ellsworth, Maine, a priest, Father John Bapst, dared to build a school. Enraged citizens blew up his chapel with gunpowder, smashed his rectory, tarred and feathered him and tried to incinerate him.

Despite this persecution, Catholics proved patriots in the Civil War as they had in the Revolution. They volunteered in large numbers on both sides. Possibly half the adult male Irish population in America, and a somewhat smaller percentage of adult male Poles, were involved. The North had some fifty Catholic generals and several "Irish brigades." The South was served by twenty Catholic general officers and one admiral.

But astonishing, and enlightening, to the Church's critics was the action of the nuns. For twenty-five years, the Protestant population had been saturated with books and pamphlets, almost universally believed, describing alleged orgies and high living in nunneries and monasteries. The nuns descended on the battlefields as angels of mercy, and by their actions disproved the vicious tales. At least six hundred sisters tended the wounded. After the Battle of Gettysburg, the Sisters of Charity at nearby Emmitsburg went to the field in a body, set up a hospital in a Methodist church and saved the lives of hundreds of wounded. Soldiers who saw the nuns at work refused thereafter to believe evil of them. For the next generation, the Catholic Church enjoyed unprecedented freedom from criticism.

But this was only a truce. Out of Clinton, Iowa, in 1887, came a new attack. By now, millions of poverty-stricken Italians and East European Catholics were fighting for an economic toehold. All the old prejudices against the Irish were amplified by an organization called the American Protective Association. The group caused national hysteria in 1893 by announcing that the Pope had ordered Catholics to rise up on St. Ignatius' feast day and exterminate the Protestant population. When the day passed without incident, the association was too discredited to survive; but a new generation had absorbed anti-Catholic fears. As a result, when the Ku Klux Klan was revitalized as an anti-Catholic force from 1915 to 1925, more than two million Americans joined.

From its start in this country, the Catholic Church had quietly gone about the job of digging in. The perhaps 23,000 Catholics here in 1789 were under the jurisdiction of the English hierarchy. Father John Carroll of Maryland insisted that survival of the Catholic Church in the new country was possible only if it was thoroughly Americanized. He envisioned a native-born clergy and hierarchy, with their own policies, Vatican-approved, in which separation of church and state would be recognized. The allegiance of American Catholics to Rome,

Carroll argued, could be only in the areas of faith and morals, not in internal politics. Along these lines, Pope Pius VI established the Diocese of Baltimore in 1789 and named John Carroll its first bishop. In 1808, Baltimore was made the first metropolitan see in the United States.

Catholics maintain that Bishop Carroll's policy has been the Catholic Church's policy ever since. Indeed, the full authoritarian power of the bishops has often been required to mold into Americans the 9,317,000 Catholic immigrants who arrived here before 1920. Foreign cultures were firmly uprooted, in an upheaval which Protestant historian William Warren Sweet acknowledges as a contribution to American city development equal to that of the Methodist circuit riders on the frontier. The policy of Americanization was costly to the Church, for great losses of membership resulted. In 1897, a Polish Catholic group centering at Scranton, Pennsylvania, left the Church and in 1904 organized the Polish National Catholic Church, which now numbers 250,000 members, and which does not recognize Papal jurisdiction. Thousands of Germans withdrew into Evangelical Protestant groups. An estimated 250,000 Irish and Italians drifted away.

So different was the Catholicism of German and Irish immigrants, and theirs in turn from that of the Greeks, Poles and Italians, that, for a generation, great administrative skill was required to prevent serious schisms. Archbishop Henry Moeller, finding Irish and German parishes in Cincinnati aloof to each other, simply transferred all the Irish pastors to German churches and vice versa, thus ending sermons in German. A priest from that area today recalls that when his mother told her Irish priest in Cincinnati that she was marrying a young German of the parish, the priest chided her, "Mary, Mary, ye be marrying outside the faith!"

The Eastern European immigrants, whose priests said Mass in Slavonic vernaculars, organized into three separate dioceses. These "Eastern Rite" Catholics, as they are called, number 462,210 and minister chiefly to Americans of Ukrainian, Eastern and Middle European backgrounds, as well as some Arabs.

The little church of Bishop Carroll grew to an organization of eighteen million members by the time James Cardinal Gibbons died in 1921. If any single man deserves the accolade "American Catholic Statesman," it is he. Of chiseled, ascetic face and graceful hands, with a smile that mirrored inner sanctity, he had a genius for friendship. He received the red hat in 1886, after the death of John Cardinal McCloskey, the first American-born "Prince of the Church." Gibbons had been a parish priest and a chaplain in the Union Army. From 1886 until 1911, he was the only native American cardinal. Born within nine hundred yards of the Baltimore cathedral that was his domain for forty-four years, he diligently cultivated good will among Catholics, Protestants and Jews. He instructed his bishops to observe Thanksgiving Day, until then strictly a Protestant custom. He refused to condemn public schools, though he was a great builder of parochial schools.

When Gibbons visited Rome in 1887, he told other members of the hierarchy that "American Catholics rejoice in our separation of church and state and I can conceive no combination of circumstances likely to arise which would make a union desirable to either church or state. . . ." He was a friend of three United States presidents, who frequently consulted him on political matters which might have produced religious conflict. At the silver jubilee of his elevation as bishop, in 1893, a letter of felicitation was sent him by President Grover Cleveland, a Presbyterian, and read by Vice-President Adlai E. Stevenson, an Episcopalian. After Gibbons had been a cardinal for twenty-five years, in 1911, President William Howard Taft escorted him to a reception in his honor in Washington. This public expression of respect amazed the British ambassador, historian James Bryce, who said that it could not have happened in his country.

Except for the New England states, the North Atlantic seaboard and Virginia, almost all of what is now the United States was first penetrated by Catholics. Their explorations broke the wilderness from Canada to the Gulf of Mexico, and from Florida to California. The first Catholic parish in what is now the United States was at Saint Augustine, Florida, founded by Spaniards in 1565. By 1640, the Franciscans had 30 missions in New Mexico. In the north, French priests were in Wisconsin by 1661, along the Illinois and Mississippi rivers by 1673, and had made a permanent settlement in Iowa by 1783. The great Junipero Serra arrived in California in 1769. He founded nine of the missions established by the Franciscans along the Pacific Coast and developed a herd of 250,000 cattle. Few perhaps recall a more permanent contribution: He kept the Russians from settling California, a feat that changed history.

There were hundreds of explorer-priests, dedicated to the task of Christianizing the Indians, among them Marquette, Hennepin, Jogues, Menard and Allouez. Not so well known, but typical of these hardy churchmen, was Pierre De Smet, a Belgian Jesuit who died in 1873. He explored the entire western half of America, an exploit greater than that of Daniel Boone. An exciting prose writer, De Smet composed accurate descriptions of the entire area from Missouri to Oregon. His information was invaluable to later settlers, for he included the habits of rattlesnakes, polecats and mountain lions, knowledge of edible and poisonous fruits and tubers, and complete navigation charts of several rivers, including the Missouri and Columbia. Thousands of immigrants used copies of Father De Smet's writings as their only guide to the wilderness of Kansas, Nebraska, Montana, Wyoming and the Rocky Mountains. He lived to hear Senator Thomas Hart Benton say of him in Congress, "Father De Smet has done more for Indian welfare and keeping them in peace and friendship with the United States than an army with banners."

The historic contributions of Catholics to the growth of the nation are, however, resented rather than applauded by some Protestants. As the Church has grown in numbers, wealth and influence, the old tensions have been revived, with increased urgency.

In 1956, four developments crystallized the suspicions and resentment: the furor over Francis Cardinal Spellman's appeal ("as a loyal citizen" in defense of

America, and as Archbishop of New York, "in solicitude for the welfare of souls entrusted to my care") to boycott the film *Baby Doll;* the pressure by Catholic laymen which forced cancellation of the film *Martin Luther* by a Chicago TV station; the church-state outburst following Justice Brennan's nomination to the Supreme Court and the pressure from several directions concerning Catholic parochial schools. These, with the Catholic stand on birth control and certain medical practices, such as eugenic sterilization and artificial insemination which the Church brands as immoral, represent the current divisive issues that separate the Catholic and the other religious communities.

Whether anyone can be simultaneously a loyal American and a loyal Catholic is the most persistent point of misunderstanding. The Protestant argument is that the Pope, being not only a spiritual leader but ruler of a 108-acre principality known as Vatican City, can if he desires tell Catholics what to do politically. Further, this argument runs, the Pope would do so if Catholics were a political majority under a Catholic President. This thesis seemed to be bolstered in 1940 by the publication of *Catholic Principles of Politics,* a book which left in Protestant minds the definite impression that, if Catholics ever got the upper hand, they would suppress other churches, destroy free speech and press and impose Catholic rule upon the nation.

The publicity over this book generated such Protestant indignation that Archbishop John T. McNicholas issued this statement in 1948: "We deny absolutely and without qualification that the Catholic bishops of the United States are seeking a union of church and state,

by any endeavors whatsoever, either proximately or re-
motely. If, tomorrow, Catholics constituted a majority
in our country, they would not seek a union of church
and state. . . ."

But Protestants, led by the magazine *Christian
Century,* refused to accept this as final. The Pope, they
said, had not spoken; and he was the only one who
could pledge for the entire Church. Actually, under
Church law and tradition, the Pope cannot make utter-
ance on such matters. Each American bishop rules his
own diocese, subject only to supervision and ratification
of his decisions by the Vatican. The Pope may speak
for the Church only on matters of faith and morals, and
then only to the entire Church, not to the American or
any other segment. Catholic policies in Spain and South
America, often deplored by Protestants, are not dictates
of the Pope but policies of the native hierarchies. In
America, bishops often have contradictory policies in
different dioceses, and they very often disagree among
themselves.

On the church-state issue, there is no evidence to
support the Protestant thesis—except the actions of
overzealous or fanatic individuals. Where Catholics have
a majority of the population, as in Rhode Island, or
are in control of power, as in the AFL-CIO, they have
not disturbed the status quo. It is significant that,
although the Church has an organization to cover almost
every phase of American life (book clubs, veterans'
clubs, National Council of Catholic Women, National
Council of Catholic Men, Boy Scouts, Girl Scouts, Catholic Youth Organization, Knights of Columbus, sodal-
ities, confraternities, etc.), it has never formed a Catholic

political party as is commonly done in Europe. Nor is
the Democratic party, as is often claimed, in effect the
Catholic party—today less than ever, according to several analyses of the 1952 and 1956 elections.

Contemporary Protestant theologians of the stature
of Reinhold Niebuhr, and the Jewish scholar Will Herberg, agree with Catholic scholars that the Catholic
Church in America has found its destiny under the
American Constitution, and that the church-state ruckus
is a dead issue. Herberg, a sociologist and former research expert for the Ladies Garment Workers Union,
recently expressed the opinion that Protestant fears of
Catholic power stem primarily from the shocked reali-
zation that the 275-year-old Protestant monopoly of
American tradition has now ended. Protestants do not
like to concede, Herberg said, that the Catholic Church
is here to stay.

Dr. Niebuhr has noted that many people do not
realize the tremendous stabilizing power of the Catholic
Church in combatting such forces as nazism and communism.

Protestants concede the Pope's right to establish a
code of conduct *for Catholics.* The clash occurs when
Catholic pressure is applied to make United States law
or observance conform to Catholic dogma, thus im-
posing the Catholic interpretation of the moral law on
non-Catholics. Catholic churchmen rejoin that such
pressures, when applied, are merely exercises of the
political right of individuals to protect American morality, just as Prohibition was imposed on the entire nation
in 1920, although most Catholics were opposed to it.
They argue that the strongest political pressures in the

field of personal conduct have been Protestant motivated: the blue laws of New England, the limitations on Sunday amusement, the curbing of prostitution, the banning of bingo and slot machines. All these are restrictions on personal liberty, enacted into law by a majority of the citizens. Catholics feel that they also have the right of every citizen to raise moral issues and to work for their enactment into law.

One acute point of friction involves the Church's voice in censorship, a phenomenon only thirty years old but increasing in intensity as Catholics grow stronger and more vocal. In an encyclical in September, 1957, the late Pope Pius XII called for an extension of Catholic censorship to include not only motion pictures but radio and television as well. The Pope exhorted the episcopacy "not only to exercise a watchful care but also to use positive action and authority."

The Catholic decision that certain films, books and magazines are "sinful" irritates non-Catholics because it not only represents a threat to freedom, but also poses a moral superiority that seems self-righteous. The Catholic attitude on birth control is controversial for these same reasons.

Patrick Joseph Cardinal Hayes touched off the censorship controversy during the 1920's when, as Archbishop of New York, he declared war on obscene pulp magazines and books. The Cardinal anticipated what is now a deep-seated feeling on the part of many Catholics, and some non-Catholics, namely, that moral values in the United States are collapsing rapidly, and that something must be done to correct this situation.

The tactics employed in the censorship, however, have often been more earnest than wise. The Church has been both embarrassed and damaged in the process. Much thought has been given this subject by eminent Catholics, both lay and clerical. While conceding the Church's obligation to work for decency in America as a whole, these thinkers conclude that Catholic tactics in censorship have frequently been impetuous, emotional and inept.

One lay view, expressed facetiously by drama critic Walter Kerr, a Catholic, is this: "I sometimes think that, if a dutiful Catholic correlated all the gratuitous advice that is given him on the subject of entertainment and conscientiously abided by it, he would have no choice but to spend his evenings in the nearest bar."

The Jesuit scholar Father John Courtney Murray sees imprudent censorship by Catholic citizen-groups as dangerous, "lest the Church itself be identified in the public mind as a power association. The identification is injurious; it turns into a hatred of the faith." He continues: "Our purpose is to stand before the world as men and women of faith, and therefore of reason, too, whose reliance is on the methods of reason and not of force. . . ."

Many—perhaps most—Catholics agree with Father Murray. But, as he himself pointed out, the harm is done in the use made of censorship by local fanatics. ". . . The zealot," he wrote in the November 3, 1956, issue of the Jesuit magazine *America,* "at times fails to see how his zeal for results may betray him into the use of methods that will in turn betray his cause."

A month later, certain zealots in Chicago forced

Station WGN-TV to cancel a Christmas-week showing of the film *Martin Luther*. There are more Catholics in the Archdiocese of Chicago than in any other single area of America. This protest was a laymen's uprising, and it acutely embarrassed the archdiocesan authorities.

Most authorities agree that the school question will continue to be the big conflict of the immediate future. Catholic schools were set up in America for two reasons: first, to protect Catholic youth from the Protestant historical viewpoint, which was universal in public and private schools; second, to perpetuate the language and customs of foreign-language immigrants, particularly the Germans. About 1884, the Irish began to demand parochial schools for a further reason: Their children were often abused and discriminated against by their classmates.

Until the mid-1850's, school texts and books for juveniles delineated only the Protestant versions of the Reformation. The Spanish Inquisition was depicted as representative of the Catholic Church. The King James Bible was read without acknowledgment that the Douay and the Vulgate versions existed. There was not even a celebration of Christmas as we know it now. As late as 1870, school children in parts of Massachusetts were deliberately kept in class on Christmas day to discourage "popish" observances.

Once under way, the parochial system spread phenomenally. Currently, according to the Official Catholic Directory, there are 258 Catholic colleges and universities, 498 seminaries, 2,372 high schools, 9,738 elementary schools, and more under construction. And still one out of every two Catholic children attends public school. The elementary schools alone require 76,833 teachers, of whom 67,477 belong to religious orders, and the total teaching force, including lay workers, exceeds 130,000. Operating costs, including interest on debt, exceed $2 billion annually. More than $10 billion has been spent on new construction and renovation since World War II. Such outlays of money are an extra burden on Church members, since Catholics must pay their share of the public-school taxes as well as the total support of their own institutions.

True, they can cut corners. The nuns and brothers who teach receive only their subsistence. Some Catholic schools have packed 50 or more youngsters into a classroom. Even so, the per-pupil cost has risen to between $90 and $100 a year on the elementary level and to $160 in high schools, not counting construction and interest on debt. Despite this financial burden, 90 per cent of the new Catholic parishes established since 1946 have erected their school ahead of their permanent church. The demand is from the laity. In September, 1956, dozens of mothers stood in line all night to enroll their children in the Park Forest, Illinois, parochial school, because only half of those eligible could be admitted.

The vaulting population and the high cost of education have already increased Catholic pressure for at least "fringe benefits" from the general public. Catholics point out that if there were no parochial schools, the already acute public-education problem would be complicated by the influx of another 3,400,000 students, necessitating billions of dollars of additional tax burden. In some states, school-bus transportation, lunchroom subsidies, distributions from government surplus farm products and free textbooks have been granted. But there, in the face of several United States Supreme Court decisions, the assistance ends. Whether the Church should go farther and campaign for relief from public-school taxation or, better, for the recognition of its schools as entitled to public support, is a question on which even the bishops do not agree. Some of them argue that public support would inevitably mean public supervision, thus destroying the unique character of parochial education.

Like the public schools, the parochial schools in the past few years have faced the problem of racial integration. Here, a distinct contribution has been made to racial justice. The famous Supreme Court decision of 1954 did not require compliance from church schools. However, in ten of the Southern states, parochial-school integration has been initiated, after forthright action on the part of several bishops. Archbishop Robert E. Lucey of San Antonio was compelled to issue a sharp pastoral letter before securing compliance from his white laymen. Archbishop Joseph F. Rummel of New Orleans began integration in 1958, despite severe antagonism climaxed by the burning of a fiery cross on his lawn.

Catholic doctrine has never drawn a color line. Many orders of priests and nuns have Negro members. James A. Healy, a mulatto, was Bishop of Portland, Maine, for twenty-five years. Two of his brothers were priests, and Patrick, a Jesuit, served for nine years as president of Georgetown University. One of the few fields in which Catholic clergy co-operate with Protestants is that of race relations. The Catholic Interracial

Movement, organized in 1934, now has thirty Interracial Councils in large cities.

The largest problem now facing the Church in America is an internal one: what to do about the "ghetto" attitude, the Catholic's withdrawal into his own parallel society. For the most part, Catholics are reluctant to leave the friendly security of church-centered activity. Believing theirs to be the true church, Catholics do not participate in non-Catholic services or in any activity that might indicate a compromise of their basic religious beliefs. They choose to remain within their own Church, their own schools and associations.

The Catholic emergence in the labor movement was logical. Catholics have a majority among the workers; therefore, they have provided much of the leadership. George Meany, president of the AFL-CIO, is a Catholic. So, too, have been the last three secretaries of labor. Priests who enter labor controversies, as did Father John M. Corridan on the New York water front, receive only praise.

In politics, the atmosphere is different. There are now ten Catholic United States senators and seventy-five representatives in Congress, a number exceeded only by the Methodists. There has even been a priest in Congress: Father Gabriel Richard, delegate of Michigan Territory from 1823 to 1825, who was remembered for the largest silver shoe buckles ever worn by a member. There have been many Catholic mayors and governors. But Catholics are painfully aware that the highest office in the land has been denied them because of their religion. Further, the actions of Catholic politicians are scrutinized constantly by Protestant watchdogs for evidence that they are voting as Catholics rather than as representatives of their constituents. Even McCarthyism was accused of being Church-directed, though the methods of the late Wisconsin senator were criticized as sharply inside the Church as out of it. Many bright young Catholics, discouraged by the political limitations imposed on them, have concluded that the rewards are not worth the abuse, and have sought careers elsewhere.

Nor is there much hope, Catholics feel, of acceptance in another generation. For 25 years, the ratio of Catholics to the total population remained roughly constant: 23 per cent Catholic, 70.8 per cent Protestant, 3.1 Jewish, 3.1 per cent other. Between 1958 and 1960, the number of Roman Catholics increased to 26.1 per cent. Even the 120,000 conversions to Catholicism each year are largely offset by withdrawals. The postwar baby boom has also been adverse, since it appears that Protestants are multiplying faster than Catholics, in the ratio of six to five.

Thus there is nothing in the offing to overcome the Catholic "withdrawal" psychology.

The younger generation of Catholic theologians argue that if Catholics broke from their self-imposed shell and took a more active part in all phases of American life, Protestants would soon realize that Catholics were no different from themselves—except in religious observance. Then, they feel, the walls of separation would come tumbling down and the bickering would end. There would always be differences of outlook and minor friction, but Catholics at least would be accepted for what they are—the loyal Americans which, time and again, they have proved themselves to be.

7

The Eastern Orthodox

FOLLOWERS of the Eastern Orthodox Church consider it a fourth major faith in America, of equal standing with the Protestant, Roman Catholic and Jewish religions. It is an ancient church of early Christendom that is only now becoming truly established as part of American life.

The Orthodox faith emphasizes the continuing concept of a church as it was created by Christ's original followers and by the Church Fathers of the first three centuries of the Christian era. It is a deeply mystic religion, marked by the Mediterranean peoples' love of symbolism and ritual, appealing to the physical senses through art and music. Its followers number about 3,000,000 in the United States. There are more than 150,000,000 Eastern Orthodox Christians in the world, making them the second largest Christian communion.

The splendor of the Orthodox service is essentially Byzantine. The Divine Liturgy, as the Mass is called, was revised by Saints Basil and John Chrysostom in the fourth century. The body of Divine Revelation, to Orthodox believers, includes both the Bible and the Holy Tradition established by the seven great Ecumenical Councils between A.D. 325 and A.D. 787.

Orthodox believers consider themselves the guardians of unadulterated Christianity. They build their churches to resemble jewel boxes, as reliquaries of the most precious of all gems, the original faith. Brilliant murals cover the church walls. A golden screen illumined with icons guards holy doors through which the glittering, candle-lighted altar beckons its promise of eternal life. Priests and deacons chant the Liturgy, and are answered by cantors or choirs. The fragrance of incense is everywhere. The pageantry is enhanced by richly robed priests and acolytes, who bear vessels and emblems of gold and the Gospels in jeweled bindings.

Few Americans, other than Orthodox Christians, know much about the Eastern Orthodox Church except to recall that in A.D. 1054 the followers of orthodox Christianity, until then united, divided into the Church of Rome and the Church of the East. After that time, the Roman Church spread throughout western Europe while the other segment, calling itself "Orthodox" (from the Greek words meaning "true belief") nourished the Christians of the Middle East, the Balkans, the northeastern Mediterranean and Russia. Only one Christian people of Latin origin, the Rumanians, adhered to Orthodoxy; the remainder allied themselves with Rome. Latin became the language of the Roman Church, whereas the policy of Eastern Orthodoxy at that time was to employ Greek or Church Slavonic.

Eastern Orthodoxy became the official state religion of Greece, Russia, Serbia, Bulgaria and Rumania. These state churches were independent of each other, each with its own synod and a hierarch who was called, depending on his authority, either a patriarch, metropolitan or archbishop. All these churches employed the same Divine

Liturgy in translation from the original Greek and espoused the same Holy Tradition. They all acknowledged the Patriarch of Constantinople as their spiritual leader, since Constantinople (now Istanbul) had been the center of Eastern Orthodoxy since A.D. 330. Orthodoxy, therefore, is united in spirit and in doctrine, but is divided in language, national politics and old-country loyalties.

These ethnic divisions have complicated greatly the Church's development in America. Orthodox immigrants naturally desired to affiliate with the same hierarchy that had served them — in their own language — at home. In consequence, Orthodoxy in America today is divided into 23 different groups. Some are independent of foreign ties; others are under old-country jurisdictions. The Greek-Americans form the largest body with 1,150,000 adherents. There are three Russian constituencies totaling more than 810,000 worshipers, of whom 755,000 are in the Russian Orthodox Greek Catholic Church of America. The others range from 200,000 of Serbian extraction, 130,000 Ukrainians, 100,000 Carpatho-Russians, 80,000 Syrians and 50,000 Rumanians, to a small group of Estonians and Latvians.

The first Eastern Orthodox hierarchy in the United States was established on the West Coast. In 1794, eight monks from a Russian monastery founded an Orthodox mission on Kodiak Island, which then, together with all the Aleutian Islands and Alaska, belonged to the Russian Empire. By 1824, almost all the Aleuts were Orthodox converts. Father John Veniaminoff compiled a grammar for the Aleutian language and translated the Divine Liturgy, the catechism and Saint Matthew's Gospel, a ten-year labor completed in 1834. Named Bishop of Alaska in 1840, Father John built a cathedral in Sitka in 1848, a Russian-spired building that is still in use.

After the Americans' purchase of Alaska, Russian Orthodoxy spread down the coast. In 1872, the Alaskan bishop moved his seat to San Francisco. In 1905, due to increasing immigration of Russian Orthodox believers on the Eastern Seaboard, the Russian church centered its administration in New York City and became an archdiocese under the Holy Synod of Russia.

Although the Russians established the first Eastern Orthodox hierarchy in America, there had been scattered immigration of Greeks and other Orthodox nationalities. A Greek-language church, Holy Trinity, was founded in New Orleans in 1866. Actually, Greek Orthodox worship had been observed on the East Coast much earlier. In colonial times an Englishman, Dr. Andrew Turnbull, had founded the settlement of New Smyrna in Florida, to which he lured Minorcan and Greek laborers in 1767. He treated his colonists so harshly that they revolted and fled to Saint Augustine, where about six hundred were settled by 1777.

The Levantines, the Greeks, the Rumanians and the Slavs were late arrivals in the United States. The bulk of them came here between 1880 and 1921. Many, except the Greeks, were recruited abroad by agents of American heavy industry. At first, they had no intention of settling permanently; they planned to return home with enough money to buy a farm. Most of them were single men who crowded into boardinghouses — often seventy-five to one hundred in a house that could scarcely accommodate twenty. Unorganized, bewildered by the English tongue, they were often exploited by their employers. Few ever achieved their dream of returning home rich.

These immigrants of Eastern Orthodox faith were kept from being swallowed up in the mass of American life by their religious tradition. The boardinghouses naturally attracted men from the same region, often from the same village in the old country. Huddled together, they organized a parish and sought a priest from their native land. The church then became the social and spiritual center of their lives. As they settled down, most of them married in the faith, further strengthening their religious communities. About sixty per cent of all Orthodox churches in the United States were established in this fashion between 1900 and 1920.

The Orthodox Church had no strong religious administration to guide and unify these parishes. The mother-country hierarchies gave some long-range assistance by sending priests and financial support. But the foreign patriarchs were reluctant to establish jurisdictions — in some cases, because the membership appeared to be transient; in others, because the Russians already had an organization, and it violated Orthodox canon law to establish parallel hierarchies in the same territory. The Russian archbishop in America had more than he could do to keep up with his own burgeoning Russian-speaking flocks. By 1916, the Russians alone had about 343 parishes and 465,000 adherents from New England across Ohio, Indiana and Illinois to California and Alaska.

Thus, except for the Russian-speaking parishes, the Orthodox churches developed as strong local organizations ruled by their laymen. They established parochial schools to preserve old-country languages, customs and religious traditions. In addition to their church centers, they sought guidance and solidarity from their newspapers and their social clubs. Many publications sprang up. Typical of them is the Greek language paper *Atlantis,* founded in New York in 1894.

The social and mutual-aid clubs, strongly church-centered, gradually replaced the boardinghouse coteries and became national fraternities. The largest of them, the Greek-American Ahepa, founded in 1922, requires its members to become American citizens and uses only the English language in its meetings. In 1939, the Junior Order of Ahepa published an English translation of the Divine Liturgy for a new Greek-American generation to whom Greek is no longer a native tongue. Ahepa also encouraged political activity and became such a force that Harry S. Truman, while President, joined it in a White House ceremony. Largely as a result of Ahepa's work, *Atlantis* in 1959 estimated that more than one thousand Greek-Americans were candidates for public office in that year.

The second generation of all the Orthodox nationalities climbed rapidly from the ranks of unskilled labor. By 1917, there were probably 1,400,000 Eastern Orthodox believers in the United States, in some 700 prosperous parishes. They had advanced sufficiently to start promoting the idea of a united church. But the Russian Revolution blew the idea apart. When the Patriarch of

Moscow became a captive of the Communists, all branches of American Orthodoxy immediately saw a danger to themselves. Because the Russians had the only archdiocese in America, it was feared that the Communists might attempt to gain nationwide control and then compel the parishes to serve the Communist cause.

The reaction of the American Orthodox faithful was immediate and violent. Almost to a man, they repudiated such dictation. But this left them even more isolated from a central church authority and from missionary financial support. A bishop sent from Soviet Russia in 1926 seized Saint Nicholas Cathedral in New York, in effect capturing the archdiocese, and launched litigation that is still before the courts.

But the seizure was an empty victory. Only two Russian parishes accepted the Communist bishop. The remainder organized the independent Russian Orthodox Greek Catholic Church of America, which won immediate allegiance from virtually all the Russian-speaking parishes at that time existing in the United States and Alaska.

Here was an opportunity for American Eastern Orthodoxy to round up all its isolated allegiances into one great national synod. Such an attempt was made, but it failed. The old-country loyalties were too strong. Instead, the parishes consolidated along language lines.

The largest group, the Greeks, had appealed earlier to the Holy Synod of Greece to extend its jurisdiction to them. In response, Metropolitan Meletios Metaxakis was sent to the United States in 1918. When Meletios took the post of Ecumenical Patriarch at Constantinople in 1922, the Archdiocese of North and South America was established. It now has five United States auxiliary bishops and an archbishop in New York. The present spiritual leader of all Eastern Orthodox bodies, Patriarch Athenagoras in Constantinople, was Archbishop of the American Greek Church from 1930 to 1948.

Some of the Ukrainians established self-governing dioceses in America. The Syrians accepted the jurisdiction of the Patriarch of Antioch. Several other groups allied with the state church of their homelands, only to fall into new difficulties when their sponsors disappeared behind the Iron Curtain. Such action forced the Rumanians and Albanians to break their administrative ties with mother-country episcopates and thus become independent American bodies.

During this turbulent period, the Protestant Episcopal Church helped save many Eastern Orthodox parishes from disintegration. Orthodox congregations continued their services in Episcopal buildings while possession of their own properties was in court dispute. Trinity Episcopal Church in New York remodeled its Saint Augustine Chapel at a cost of forty thousand dollars as a temporary cathedral for the Russian-Americans ousted from Saint Nicholas. This gesture helped the Russians to maintain an independent metropolitan district until they acquired their present cathedral on Second Street in New York. These brotherly Episcopal acts greatly influenced the Eastern Orthodox Church's emergence, after World War II, from religious isolation into vigorous membership in the local, National and World Councils of Churches.

Eastern Orthodoxy feels it has a strong contribution to make to all Christianity. In the words of Archbishop Iakovos, Greek primate in America, "the riches of its faith, worship and order, and of its spiritual and ascetic life and experience," are accents which the Protestant denominations might well restudy. Orthodox beliefs, which include seven Sacraments, are based on the thesis that God created the world; God the Son (Jesus) perfected this creation on earth; and God the Holy Ghost works through mortals to give Christianity life and meaning, and mankind eternal life.

The Divine Liturgy is the most elaborate and colorful in Christendom, lasting from sixty minutes to three hours, depending on the occasion. It takes place behind the icon screen that separates the nave and sanctuary. The icons are flat images of Christ, the Blessed Virgin, the Apostles and Saints. The Liturgy is always sung, and is a dialogue between the priest and lay voices. No Orthodox service is possible without at least one layman present to make the responses. Except among some of the Greeks, the Liturgy is unaccompanied by musical instruments, and the Orthodox churches take great pride in their choirs and cantors. Highly trained ensembles of up to one hundred voices are the rule.

The Sacrament of Holy Communion is obligatory for laymen once a year, during Holy Week. It is taken after Confession, which is a Sacrament in its own right and not just a preamble to Communion. There is increasingly a return to the more normal practice of frequent Communion, every Sunday or once a month. To underscore the belief that all men become brothers in Christ, the unconsecrated portion of the bread remaining after the service is distributed to all the faithful. At various times in the matins that precede the Liturgy, and during the Liturgy itself, the priest walks through the congregation, swinging an incense-smoking censer, and blesses the congregation and the icons.

Many Orthodox customs differ from the practices of other Christian churches. Married men are accepted to the priesthood, but priests may not marry once they have been ordained. Most Orthodox priests are family heads, but bishops may be elected only from among the celibate clergy. Baptism is by triple immersion during a colorful sacrament that is followed immediately by Confirmation, even though the baptized person is an infant.

The parish organization is basically democratic. Some parishes even call their own priests. Bishops are appointed by their respective synods after being recommended by church conventions that both priests and laymen attend.

Church finance also is unusual. Every family head is assessed fixed dues, which are the same for each member on the argument that everyone is equal in God's sight and must share equal responsibility. These levies do not begin to meet expenses. Therefore anonymous gifts are solicited by plate collections, two or more of which may be taken at each service for special projects such as the support of the parochial school, a building

fund, or the bishop. Most members respond generously
to these extra appeals according to their means, but receive no parish credit for such contributions. Revenues
also are augmented by social events—picnics, banquets,
dances and religious festivals, many of which are me-
morialized by a souvenir booklet containing advertising.
Large sums are collected by the sale of votive candles,
and from such personal services as weddings, funerals,
memorials, baptisms, Te Deums and thanksgivings.

Eastern Orthodox churches tolerate limited divorce,
but discourage birth control. However, family planning
is practiced by some of the younger generation.

The church calendar differs from that of Western
Christian bodies. Some synods use the old-style Julian
calendar, which is thirteen days behind the modern
Gregorian system. But the crux of timing is the date of
Easter. In the West, Easter falls on the first Sunday after
the full moon on or after March 21. However, among the
Orthodox, Easter may not precede the Jewish Passover
and therefore is often postponed. Easter may coincide
with the Western season, as it does six times between
1950 and 1970, or it may fall from one to several weeks
later. This affects the dates of all other religious festivals pegged to the Easter date. Orthodoxy has no Ash
Wednesday. Its Easter Lenten season lasts for seven
weeks, during which fasting is so rigorous that not even
dairy products may be consumed.

Home worship is at the heart of the Eastern Orthodox
tradition. Most Orthodox households contain a corner
sanctuary lighted by a hanging lamp, in which an icon of

Christ is central. Over most beds is an icon or cross. Orthodox churchmen claim that the low incidence of criminality among Orthodox believers is due to this strong family-worship tradition.

Eastern Orthodoxy as it exists today in the United States may well be illustrated by Saints Constantine and Helen Greek Orthodox Church in Chicago. Founded with a parochial school in 1910 on Chicago's South Side, it followed its people in the second generation to a better neighborhood close to Jackson Park and the Lake Michigan water front, and now ministers to 1,500 families. Services and the Sunday-school Liturgy are in Greek, with a sermon in English. The parochial grammar school of 350 students teaches in English in the morning and in Greek, with different instructors, in the afternoon. Most of the parishioners are middle-class and self-employed. There are a few millionaires. No members are on relief rolls, there is no juvenile-delinquency problem, and there is almost no divorce. The families average three children.

Father Basil Gregory, the thirty-five-year-old priest, is a native American. This is significant, for most Eastern Orthodox churches now emphasize an American-born priesthood trained in one of the United States seminaries supported by the Greeks, the independent Russians, the Carpatho-Russians and the Ukrainians. Father Gregory loyally upholds the Greek liturgical language and also the ancient tradition except in one respect — he wears no beard. But due to the democratic lay control, protected by a written constitution, innovations are creeping in. Organ music accompanies the Divine Liturgy. Pews, unheard of in the old country, are provided. There is a strong woman's auxiliary, unknown except in America. Also, there is a feeling among most younger members that an English-language Liturgy and a consolidated archdiocese of some kind are logical future developments. The parish works closely with the ten other Greek Orthodox churches in Chicago, and those of other Orthodox language communions, in city-wide religious observances and interfaith enterprises.

An example of Eastern Orthodoxy of the future may well be shaping up in Cleveland, Ohio. Here, at latest count, there are 16 Orthodox parishes with 10 new churches under construction. They serve 90,000 members who are under seven different ecclesiastical jurisdictions. Yet all of them work happily together in an Eastern Orthodox Welfare Council which sponsors a personal-service department, a credit union, adult and Americanization education, a summer camp and a Sunday-school teacher-training program. The youth organizations of all branches are active in the Council of Eastern Orthodox Youth Leaders of America. This association, organized only in 1954, had by 1960 a national membership of 56,000 dedicated to breaking down the divisive elements within the Church.

In Cleveland, the language barriers are crumbling. Three Russian Orthodox churches have a Divine Liturgy in English, in common with about ten per cent of all United States Russian parishes. Saint Ephrem Albanian Orthodox Church and Saint Mary's Rumanian Orthodox Church have English sections in their Liturgies, as do the Serbians and Ukrainians. The Syrians have made the transition from Arabic to English, and the Carpatho-Russians from Church Slavonic to English. Only the Greeks have not made concessions to English in the Liturgy, but they may have English sermons and English-language Sunday schools.

The priest of Saint Mary's Rumanian Orthodox Church, Father Vasile Hategan, is chairman or initiator of a half-dozen national organizations for unification of the faith, and a leader in the Cleveland experiment. Like most unification leaders, Father Hategan would make all the churches bilingual and carefully preserve the strength of the old-country customs and traditions to enrich all of American Orthodoxy. This attitude is widely endorsed by the younger generation in all branches, but has not yet found general acceptance among the older worshipers and among most of the bishops.

Meanwhile, Eastern Orthodoxy campaigns for recognition as a fourth major faith. Since World War II, some twenty state legislatures and the United States Congress have passed resolutions accepting this thesis, and the importance of Eastern Orthodoxy as a growing religious and cultural force in America is recognized by all faiths. Military identification tags now bear the symbol "EO" for the first time, and Eastern Orthodox chaplains now serve with the armed forces. A milestone in the recognition of Eastern Orthodoxy was reached when an Orthodox archbishop was invited to lead a prayer at the second inauguration of President Eisenhower.

This recognition is important to the Eastern Church in its role as a unifier of Christianity. Orthodox Christians conceive of themselves as members of the church which produced organized Christianity and gave the world the New Testament. They follow that tradition which preserved the message of the Apostles for one thousand years and is today basic to all Christian faiths. Now Eastern Orthodoxy would like nothing better than to assume leadership in reconciling Christian differences, in answer to the Apostle John's prayer that "they all may be one."

8

The Episcopalians

THE EPISCOPAL CHURCH in the United States has always attracted the carriage trade. In almost every community, it is the fashionable setting for weddings and funerals. But amid the Ivy League-suited men and the women in furs who long have characterized Episcopalians as scions of hereditary position, a new element is noticeable: the plain middle class. In the present generation, Episcopalianism in America finally is becoming the denomination that its theology has always intended it to be: a truly universal church appealing to all kinds of Christians.

This transition is by no means complete. Vestigial customs persist in many of the best-known silk-stocking Episcopal preparatory schools, in a hundred church-related secondary day schools and in a generous enclave of entrenched parishes in the East and South, where snobbery is still sometimes equated with religion. But generally speaking, anyone today is sincerely welcome to the Episcopal Communion who finds spiritual quickening in the venerable tradition, the prayer book and the liturgy of the Church, all of which uniquely characterize the denomination as one in spirit with Roman Catholicism. The Church is surging forward with a dynamism previously unknown to it in all its long history on the American continent.

It is among the fastest-growing faiths, in percentage terms, in the United States. In 1950, there were 2,540,-548 baptized persons in the Church; in 1957, there were 3,274,867. Most of these new members are mature adults reared in other denominations—or in none at all. More than half the new candidates for the priesthood were born into evangelical homes, such as Methodist and Baptist, or into Roman Catholic. There are 4,000 more lay readers (laymen who conduct church services and administer parishes and missions) than there are priests, and most of them are converts.

One of the largest Episcopal churches in America now is Saint Philip's in Harlem, a congregation of three thousand Negroes. Eight of the twelve vestrymen (ruling laymen) at Grace Church in Detroit are Negroes. There is a Japanese-language parish in Seattle. Many Spanish-speaking missions flourish in New York City, in the Southwest and in California. Saint Luke's Church in Allen Park, Michigan, is composed almost entirely of assembly-line workers in the auto industry.

The resurgence of Episcopalianism is a phenomenon of modern American religious life. It indicates a distinct trend toward a more traditional point of view. The Protestant Episcopal Church is Protestant in that it is divorced from the Roman Catholic hierarchy, and thus is free to place the Bible first in its theology and permit its lay members to share in its leadership. In all other important respects, it remains Catholic. Its *Book of Common Prayer* is basically an English translation of the Mass. The emphasis on a liturgy that binds members into a religious community transcending themselves, the sacraments and creeds, the ministry of the Holy Ghost, the mystery of the Eucharist (Holy Communion)—all are in the great Catholic spirit.

The Church is called Protestant because it protests against changes in the faith since the days of the Apostles. It is named Episcopal because the Greek New Testament uses the term *episkopos,* meaning "overseer" or "bishop." Hence the English derivative "episcopal," meaning "pertaining to bishops." This emphasis on the bishop is vital to the Church's theology, since only the bishops may ordain clergy and confirm new members. The purpose of these exclusive prerogatives is to prevent adulteration of the faith by innovations that are not Biblical in spirit. Thus Episcopalianism is a bridge between the Reformation denominations that have shed Catholic tradition entirely, and the Roman Catholic, Old Catholic and Eastern Orthodox faiths.

There are wide variations in observance within the Episcopal community. Some parishes, called Anglo-Catholic, are scarcely distinguishable from Roman Catholic churches in their emphasis on confession and absolution, their burning of incense and anointing with holy oil. There are also Episcopal orders of monks and nuns. Disciplines and fasts are prescribed. These examples point up the fact that, except for its separation from Rome, the denomination is a Catholic church, theologically and liturgically. King Henry VIII of England very likely never intended it to be much else when he divorced his national church from Rome. The transition was from a Roman Catholic to an English (Anglican) Catholic organization. In this country, after the Revolution, this became in turn the independent Protestant Episcopal Church.

The English Church was identified with the American colonies from the earliest settlements. The first white child born in America, Virginia Dare, was baptized an Anglican in the Roanoke Island, Virginia, colony of 1587. When Jamestown, Virginia, was settled in 1607, the Reverend Robert Hunt spread a ship's sail between several trees and under this canopy held regular masses until a small wooden church could be built. In 1613, the Reverend Alexander Whitaker baptized the Indian, Pocahontas, and solemnized her marriage to John Rolfe.

As the colonies developed, the English Church became the state religion in Virginia, Maryland, Georgia, North and South Carolina and the environs of New York City. This meant that all the people in those commonwealths were taxed to support the official church, whether they belonged to it or not. Since Episcopalians were in the minority everywhere except in Virginia, these assessments were deeply resented.

Even with taxation, the Church did not pay its way, except in Virginia and Maryland. From England, a missionary organization called the Society for the Propagation of the Gospel sustained more than two hundred American parishes. In addition, the Society brought culture to the colonies by supporting many schoolmasters and establishing scores of parochial libraries. Its founder, Dr. Thomas Bray, set up fifty public lending libraries in America and sent them thirty-four thousand books.

In sharp contrast to the Puritans and other Reformation groups who kept their members under Spartan discipline and made churchgoing the foremost act of colonial life, the Episcopalians were indulgent and easygoing. Their churches had steeples, crystal or brass

chandeliers and other elegances; the parishioners wore
lace and jewels. To the readings from the prayer book
were added metric psalms sung by choirs. As early as
1713, there was an organ in King's Chapel in Boston.
This heirloom, incidentally, is still in use at Saint John's
Church in Portsmouth, New Hampshire. There was a
boys' choir at Trinity Church in New York, in 1739.
Edifices were financed by the sale of pews, which then
became the exclusive property of the purchasing families,
a practice that discouraged outsiders. The royal governor often sat on a crimson-velvet throne, and after the
service would invite the priest home for a glass of wine.

The colonial Episcopalians were poorly organized.
Jurisdiction rested in the Bishop of London. For 177
years, there was no resident bishop in America. Thus
generations grew up and died without ever being confirmed in membership. The priests, answerable, practically speaking, to no one, their livings guaranteed,
were often lax or lazy. There never were half enough
clergy to supply the parishes, with the result that the
services were often read by laymen who could not administer the sacraments. Obviously, without priests or
bishops to guide them, the lay leaders ran their religious
affairs to suit themselves, sometimes with little regard
for Church law. Young men who wished to enter the
priesthood were required to go to England for ordination.
The trip cost $3,000 in today's currency, so few could
afford it. One out of every five men who embarked became a victim of shipwreck or London plague.

The American Revolution destroyed the Anglican
Church with catastrophic suddenness. Except in the

South, the Episcopalians by and large were loyal to George III, and Church law required them to pray for the royal family at every service and to display the royal coat of arms. That made them prime targets for the revolutionaries.

Many Episcopalians, laymen and clergy both, fled to Canada and England. In London, the missionary society stopped all payments, and the Bishop of London lost even his feeble contact with the Church in America. State Church taxes, of course, were abolished. Thus, the entire foundation and finance of the Anglicans collapsed overnight.

Parishes that espoused the Revolution revised the prayer book to eliminate supplications for the King. All effective Church administration ceased. King's Chapel in Boston became a Unitarian church. Of the fourteen priests in Massachusetts in 1776, most went to Nova Scotia. Paul Revere's signal lantern was hung in Boston's Christ Church, better known as "Old North." Throughout New England, Anglican clergymen were baited, stoned, pulled from their pulpits and tarred; their homes were looted and burned. John Stuart, the famous pre-Revolutionary missionary, was hounded from his post among the Indians in New York State, sent to prison and later chased into Canada. Ebenezer Diblee was continually harassed, but kept at his post.

Another intrepid holdout was octogenarian John Beach of Newtown, Connecticut, who continued royalist prayers throughout the war—when he was not in jail. Dr. Myles Cooper, president of Episcopal-founded King's College (now Columbia University) in New York, escaped death by slipping from his rectory while a student named Alexander Hamilton distracted a mob outside.

Despite the Tory sympathies of many Anglicans, a number of them, notably the Virginians, South Carolinians and those in Philadelphia, contributed the strongest leadership to the Revolution and the new government. Of the fifty-six signers of the Declaration of Independence, two-thirds were Episcopalians, and of the thirty-nine framers of the Constitution, two-thirds were members of the Episcopal Church. Among these Episcopal framers of the Constitution was Charles Pinckney of South Carolina, who proposed the clause on religious liberty in that document.

The company of Virginians included George Washington and Thomas Jefferson, both vestrymen; James Madison, who wrote the Bill of Rights; George Mason, who framed the declaration of rights in the Virginia constitution. Patrick Henry's famous "liberty or death" oration was delivered at Saint John's Church in Richmond, Virginia, during the Virginia convention of 1775.

Because of the Church's pro-Revolution stand in Virginia, the glebe lands (Church-owned properties whose revenues supported the priesthood) were not taken from their rectors. Among them, the priests owned 21,801 acres. Nevertheless, from being the largest pre-Revolutionary church, the Episcopalians in 1783 had been reduced to one of the smallest, with no national ties and only loose, dormant federations in Connecticut, New York, Pennsylvania, Virginia and Maryland.

Now, however, a remarkable man stepped forward who was to lead his denomination, in the short space of seven years, to a firm national organization. His name was William White, rector of both Christ Church and Saint Peter's in Philadelphia. At the outbreak of war, White was merely an assistant minister at Christ Church. When the regular priest went to England, White became pastor, and also a chaplain of the Continental Congress. His sister was the wife of Robert Morris, financier of the Revolution. With a private fortune of his own, White was able to support himself throughout the war and to hold the two Philadelphia parishes together.

When the Revolution ended, White realized that he was the only Anglican priest left in the city. It was obvious to him that, unless quick action was taken, the Anglican Church in America would never be revived. He wrote a pamphlet, addressed to all Episcopalians, arguing that the denomination reorganize, then try to procure a local bishop.

He received immediate response from the scattered, disorganized parishes. It was not all favorable. New Englanders believed that a bishop must be obtained first, and a hierarchy then organized around him. In March of 1783, the Connecticut clergy, the strongest state-church group, met and elected Samuel Seabury to be their bishop. Seabury was a native of Groton, Connecticut, a graduate of Yale and of Edinburgh University in Scotland. He had been exiled during the war. He went to England to seek recognition and consecration from the mother church.

White later rallied the remainder of the American Episcopalians. Bishops were elected for Virginia, Maryland, Pennsylvania and New York, to be ordained by the

English bishops. Only two of the four electees could make the trip to England: White, the nominee for Pennsylvania, and Samuel Provoost, rector of New York's Trinity parish.

In England, Seabury was rejected by British authorities because an oath of allegiance to the crown was still required for consecration. As an American, Seabury obviously could not take this oath. He then went to Aberdeen, to consult dignitaries of the Episcopal Church of Scotland, who were not in communion with the English Anglicans. Probably to irritate the English hierarchy, the Scottish churchmen consecrated Seabury as the first bishop of the American Episcopalians. He was promptly accepted by all the New England parishes. Three years later, White and Provoost received their credentials from the English Church.

Then, Bishop White called a general convocation of the American Anglicans in 1789. To prevent schism, he proposed that Seabury's consecration be accepted. The motion carried unanimously. White and Seabury (Provoost was unable to join them) then organized a House of Bishops, while clergy and laymen established a House of Deputies. Thus the American Church was born. Swiftly, the body also adopted a constitution, approved a prayer book and canon law. But the denomination was pitifully feeble compared with its former grandeur, with only twenty-two clergy and sixteen laymen present at this historic meeting.

The next twenty years were critical ones. Episcopalians in many areas had to learn how to support their churches, their schools, hospitals and seminaries by voluntary gifts instead of through government subsidy. They had to adjust to survival without political sponsorship, under the sharp eye of resident bishops who curbed the authority of the laymen. They also had to prove to the new republic that an Anglican hierarchy in America would not attempt to overthrow freedom of religion.

Naturally, recovery was very slow. In 1792, Thomas J. Claggett was consecrated Bishop of Maryland, in the first investiture on American soil. But he was not in charge of much: Only twenty-three clergy were present at his election. In nearby Delaware at that time, only three clergymen could be found. However, this diocese was eventually strengthened when many Swedish Lutherans embraced the Episcopal faith.

By 1820, sufficient strength had been achieved for the creation of a missionary society to finance frontier work. In 1823, a commission was formed to revise Church music and introduce hymn singing. One member of both these bodies was Francis Scott Key, who wrote "The Star-Spangled Banner."

In 1835, the Church really began to move. The General Convention consecrated bishops to work on the frontier. At that time, there were just 36,416 Episcopalians in the entire country. The early missionary bishops ranged far and suffered much. Jackson Kemper, in the Midwest, journeyed some 100,000 miles on horseback, while organizing dioceses in Missouri, Indiana, Wisconsin, Iowa and Minnesota and the first missions in Nebraska and Kansas. The diocese of Bishop Joseph C. Talbot included the territories of Dakota, Nebraska, Colorado, Utah, Montana, Wyoming and Nevada. He

needed 18 days just to ride from his home in Nebraska City, Nebraska, to the center of his diocese at
Denver. The first parish in Colorado was organized in
a Nevada City dance hall, and when Bishop Talbot arrived to confirm members, the saloons all closed in his
honor. In Idaho, the pioneer church included among
its members the town saloonkeeper.

A colorful pioneer leader was Leonidas Polk, son of
a North Carolina planter. He was created Bishop of
the Southwest in 1838. The first tour of his diocese
took five months. He found not a single Episcopal rector
west of the Mississippi along the Gulf Coast except in
Texas. The outbreak of the Civil War found Polk in
Louisiana. Because in his youth he had been graduated
from the United States Military Academy, he was commissioned a Confederate major general, and served as a
corps commander until killed at Pine Mountain in 1864.
Polk is the only recorded bishop of any faith in America
who simultaneously was an army general, except in the
corps of chaplains.

The Civil War affected the Episcopal Church very
little. It took no stand on the slavery question. The
Southern parishes edited their prayer book to include
the president of the Confederacy. Once the war was over,
the Southerners returned to the General Convention.

By World War I, Episcopalianism was established
throughout the nation as the Protestant church of the
socially prominent and of those who wanted to worship
in the Catholic tradition without alliance with Rome.
In 1915, the membership was 1,040,896, of whom 85
per cent were in the East and South, 10 per cent in the

Midwest and only five per cent in the West and Southwest. The denomination was characterized by the evangelist Billy Sunday as a "sleeping giant," gaining only 611,000 members in the 35 years between 1915 and 1950. Not until the 1950's did the giant awaken. Now he is very wide awake indeed.

A new policy of the American bishops emphasizes the problems of living. "We are well aware," says Dr. Paul Musselman, executive secretary of the Division of Urban Industrial Church Work, "that the people are looking the churches over, to see which are concerned with the problems of humanity in a space age. That church does its job best which gives members a chance to express their religion where they live."

This challenge has led the Episcopal Church far afield. In Roxbury, Massachusetts, Saint John's parish has opened a mission in a downtown store, because many people will worship in a simple building who will not enter a Gothic edifice. In New York, historic Trinity Church at the head of Wall Street has sponsored a dozen missions in several languages. Uptown, the Reverend James A. Gusweller, of the Church of Saints Matthew and Timothy, who ministers now to a neighborhood predominantly Puerto Rican, spoke out so boldly in 1958 against rent gougers and bribe-taking housing inspectors who had preyed on his flock, that he caused a city investigation of public corruption.

In Brooklyn, Archdeacon A. Edward Saunders, a former Marine Corps combat major, works on the waterfront among the longshoremen. In Seattle, Bishop Stephen F. Bayne, Jr., closed the Church of the Advent when it became one hundred per cent Negro, and relocated its one hundred families among other parishes. In Detroit, Bishop Richard S. Emrich's labor relations committee sat in on negotiations during the 1958 Dodge Motor Company strike, not as mediators but to familiarize priests of the diocese with problems of labor-management conflict.

An acute problem of Episcopalianism is that in many cities it has built huge Gothic churches and cathedrals in downtown areas which now are blighted. The original communicants have long since moved away. The districts have filled up with Southern hill folk, Puerto Ricans and factory workers. The Church, therefore, has faced a direct challenge. If it was to be a truly universal faith, it must minister to these people. It has done so. Few downtown Episcopal parishes in large cities have been abandoned. Instead, they have accommodated themselves to their environment. Detroit furnishes a classic example of this accommodation. In fifteen years, fifty-one Protestant congregations downtown have migrated to the suburbs. At the insistence of Bishop Emrich, not one of the fourteen Episcopal centers in the area has closed. Grace Church, Detroit, was a prestige parish for many years. Gradually, Negroes moved into this Virginia Park section as the original families departed. By 1952, Grace Church's membership had dropped from five hundred families to two hundred. Bishop Emrich sent in a Haitian-Negro assistant priest, Father Henri Stines. Through a seven-day-a-week program of community service, Father Stines, now rector, has built the parish back to its former size.

In Seattle, Washington, Trinity Church, once the city's most fashionable, has become a community parish. The transition shows best in the choirs. The adult singers include old-time aristocrats, one Chinese, a few Nisei, a few Negroes. The junior choir is predominantly Negro and Oriental, with a few white children.

Part of the Episcopal growth of the past decade, and its preoccupation with what the *Book of Common Prayer* calls "all sorts and conditions of men," is due to the impact of these erstwhile outsiders. Being new to the faith, they are, like the converts to any religion, the most zealous. They also have brought to Episcopalianism the missionary drive of the Baptists and Methodists. This is because they have found, in the timeless and stately Episcopal tradition, an intensely personal religious experience.

The intensity of personal Christianity in the Church is illustrated by its new priests. Hundreds of them are mature men who, responding to their discovered faith, have left careers in industry and business to devote their whole lives to Christ's service. They know the language, the thoughts and the problems of working people at first hand. As a result, they are tremendously successful as parish priests. Canon Rudolf Devik at Seattle is a former pump salesman. Dr. William B. Atkinson, assistant priest at Grace Church, Louisville, Kentucky, is chief of anatomy at the Louisville University School of Medicine during the week. John Yaryan, vicar at Saint Matthew's Church, Auburn, Washington, is a former corporation vice-president. Brigadier General Lester J. Maitland, a pioneer aviator, is priest at Saint Stephen's Church, Escanaba, Michigan.

This surge of older men is so great that two dioceses, Long Island and Detroit, have set up night schools in which candidates may read for Holy Orders. On ordination, they quit their jobs in business and the professions, and become deacons.

Other men of like enthusiasm are enrolling as lay readers. The Diocese of Olympia, Washington, alone uses 210 of them. All of them work at secular jobs during the week. On Sundays, their bishop or rector sends them to nearby missions to conduct services and head the local organization. The Church in 1958 had 12,493 lay readers. More than 600 unorganized congregations were served by them, with only occasional visits from an ordained priest.

The newcomers also have raised the Church's standard of giving. In dioceses where the converts are most numerous, generosity is most evident. For example, in Michigan, where membership has increased 40 per cent in nine years, the annual receipts have increased 232 per cent. In the State of Washington, where membership is up 60 per cent, total giving has soared 110 per cent. Much of this money is being reinvested in new United States missions. Bishop Emrich, in a 1958 report to the Home Department of the Church, estimated that the denomination will add another 800,000 communicants to its rolls before 1970.

One attraction of the Episcopal Church is its moderate position on social and moral questions. It endorses birth control and family planning. It fights alcoholism, but does not disapprove of reasonable social drinking. It has relaxed the traditional Catholic position on divorce, conceding that emotional and psychological factors may make a marriage intolerable. It throws itself into reform, but not so vigorously as to give the impression of wishing to revolutionize the social order all at once. Thus it provides an unimpassioned meeting ground for left- and right-wing positions.

American Episcopalians historically also have been leaders in the movement for reunion of all Christian believers. They themselves are a self-governing part of the worldwide Anglican Communion of 40,000,000 members. They helped to create what is now the National Council of Churches, and the former Presiding Bishop, Henry Knox Sherrill, was the foremost leader in the establishment of the World Council of Churches. They envision a day when all Protestantism will be reunited, and then will merge with the Orthodox and Roman Catholic branches into one holy and apostolic Christian brotherhood.

9

The Jews

I T IS NO ACCIDENT that about 5,250,000 Jews, nearly
half the world's Jewish population, are Americans.
Jews have had more real freedom in the United States
than they have ever had in any other country where
they have lived as a minority social-religious group in
the past 2,000 years. Except for Israel, America is the
only nation that from its beginning granted equality
under the law to Jews or permitted them full expression
of their abilities. The United States, in turn, has bene-
fited perhaps more from their productivity than has any
other nation.

Although the Jews in America are the largest and
most influential Jewish community anywhere, they did
not assume this role until recently. The turning point
came when six million European Jews were murdered
by the Nazis, and hundreds of thousands more were left
homeless. To the present day, this blood bath remains
the most shocking memory in the minds of most American Jews.

In the aftermath of the slaughter, they responded
to their new responsibilities with almost desperate energy.
With other Jews in the free world, they helped organize
a mighty effort to rescue displaced European Jews and
to shore up their refuge, Israel. In eleven years, from

1945 to 1956, American Jews contributed $900,000,000 and countless hours of hard work to this cause.

Yet, although Israel has become a state, fulfilling the Biblical prophecy that the Jewish people would one day re-establish their nation in Palestine, only a handful of American Jews have felt an urge to live there. With the establishment of Israel, twenty centuries of the "Wandering Jew" came to an end for many, but American Jews had long since found their home. They were stirred by the rebirth of Israel; sharing in it drew them closer to one another and gave many a deeper appreciation of their Jewish identity. But for most American Jews, Zionism, the dynamic world movement to establish a Jewish national home, has come to mean only a "deep concern" for the State of Israel.

Jews in the United States have been through too much, have given and received too much, to be anything but Americans.

They found here not merely tolerance but respect. The freedom to become assimilated into the prevailing secular culture was heady wine after generations of restrictions in Europe's ghettos. And with the passionate struggle for self-improvement came a source of new pride. Science and socialism shook Judaism's traditional foundations. For two generations, many Jews had increasingly neglected religious observances. Rather, they put their faith in some form of social idealism. But then came the shock of Hitler's rise to power, wartime anxiety, the cold war and the Communist persecution of Jews in Russia.

Such experiences helped inspire great numbers of American Jews to re-evaluate the importance of the Jewish religion for themselves and their children. The conflict that had once existed for many Jews—between practicing Judaism and participating in the main stream of American life—was muted. Thus, a unique pattern of Jewish life is developing in the United States. It is a pattern that unites five thousand years of tradition with three hundred years of growth and experience in a free land.

Jews were associated with the very beginnings of America. Five of Columbus's men, including the first to step ashore in the New World, were *marranos,* Jews converted to Christianity under the Spanish Inquisition. But the first significant Jewish settlement in what is now the United States started 304 years ago, with the arrival of 23 penniless refugees in New Amsterdam in September, 1654.

This group had fled Brazil after its reconquest by Portugal from Holland. They were met by two earlier arrivals, one of whom, Jacob bar Simson, became a leader of the new group. In less than ten years, they won from Peter Stuyvesant not only the right to buy real estate and engage in retail trade, but also the right to bear arms and join the militia in defense of their city.

Like Lutherans, Catholics and all other congregations except the Dutch Reform Church, Jews were prohibited from public worship; but, from the beginning, the right of a congregation to worship at home was respected. The New Amsterdam colony eventually passed into the hands of the British and became New York. The first synagogue in North America was established there by 1692. The Jews had gained the right to public worship merely by taking it, apparently without permission but also without opposition.

Meanwhile, other Jews settled elsewhere in the colonies. In 1658, one group arrived in Newport, Rhode Island, and by 1677 had purchased a cemetery. It was one of the first steps in forming the congregation that in 1763 built the beautiful Touro Synagogue, the oldest synagogue building still standing in the United States. Aaron Lopez of Newport, a leading member of this community, owned more than thirty ships and was one of the most important merchants in New England.

From Philadelphia, Jews carried on frontier trade, sending expeditions as far away as the Mississippi Valley. In 1674, Boston's first Jewish taxpayer, Rowland Gideon, was added to the rolls. In 1656, a doctor, Jacob Lumbrozo, began to practice in Maryland. About 1732, forty-three Jews from England reached Georgia and settled in Savannah. They were joined by forty others under the leadership of Samuel Nuñez, a Portuguese physician who arrived during an epidemic and promptly helped to end it.

Early Jewish immigration was limited, however, and the Jews were widely scattered. In 1790, there were not more than 2,500 in the United States. By 1800, only six congregations had built synagogues. These were in New York, Newport, Philadelphia, Savannah, Charleston, South Carolina, and Richmond, Virginia.

Yet most Jews had given themselves wholeheartedly to the Revolution. The words of Jefferson, "that all men are created equal, that they are endowed by their Creator with certain unalienable Rights," reflect Jewish concepts of social justice that date back to the fourteenth century before the Christian era. Led by the patriot Gershom Mendes Seixas, the New York congregation defiantly closed its synagogue doors when the British Army arrived. Haym Salomon of New York was condemned to death by the British for aiding the Revolution. He escaped to Philadelphia, where he became a financial broker to the Continental Congress. He floated many of the war loans. At least twenty officers in the Continental Army were Jews, notably Benjamin Nones, an infantry major under General Casimir Pulaski, and Isaac Franks, an aide to General George Washington. Benjamin Seixas, brother of Gershom, was a colonel in the New York militia, while a third brother, Abraham, was an officer with the Georgia brigade.

Inspired by the new United States Constitution, which established an actual equality such as no Jew then living had ever known, Jews played an important role in the early days of national expansion. Many put peddlers' packs on their backs and headed for the frontier; some were staked by such already prominent Jews as the Simon, Gratz and Franks families of Philadelphia. They helped open the lands that were to become West Virginia, Ohio, Kentucky, Indiana, Illinois and Missouri. They carried supplies to trappers and farmers, built gunshops, gristmills and paper and hemp mills. They were among those who launched the first packet boats on the Ohio and built the first railroad west of the Alleghenies.

When a Jewish peddler accumulated enough capital to open a store at a crossroads, he settled down. You can drive entirely across America today, eating and sleeping in towns named for their pioneering Jewish founders—from Gilman, Connecticut, and Aaronsburg, Pennsylvania, to Roseville, California, and Heppner, Oregon.

Abraham Mordecai, who was born in Pennsylvania about 1755, was one of the most colorful Jewish pioneers. During the Revolution, he fought for three years in New Jersey and Delaware. After the war, he shouldered a one hundred-pound pack, containing shoes, clothing, tinware, ammunition, ribbons and laces, and headed south and west. By 1785, he had settled in Montgomery County, Alabama, where he dealt in skins, furs, pinkroot, hickory-nut oil and other products he gained by trade with the Indians among whom he lived. His pack trains made frequent trips to Augusta and Pensacola, while his canoes carried goods to New Orleans and Mobile. Pickett's *History of Alabama* credits Mordecai with founding the city of Montgomery. In 1802, with two others, he built Alabama's first cotton gin at Weatherford's race track. When he was no youngster, he joined the United States forces in Georgia to fight in the war of 1812. When he was past eighty, the Federal Government separated him from his Indian wife when it moved the Creeks west. He died in 1850 in a hut near Dudleyville, Alabama, among his Indian friends.

As America moved westward, the Jewish spirit was in the vanguard. Judah Touro, of the Newport, Rhode Island, family, established in New Orleans the Touro Infirmary, which was destined to become one of the largest hospitals in the South. Touro had fought under General Andrew Jackson and had been seriously wounded. Solomon Nunes Carvalho was artist, photographer and diarist on Colonel John C. Frémont's fifth and final expedition, a harrowing search for a new railroad route through the mountains to the Pacific. On his arrival in Los Angeles in 1854, Carvalho discovered a small Jewish community there and helped found its first charitable organization.

Captain Uriah P. Levy, who served the United States Navy during the War of 1812, became commodore of the American Mediterranean squadron in 1859, after having fought to avoid being shelved by the Navy. His struggle was a classic example of how American Jews sometimes had to insist on their right to serve the new nation. Earlier, as a lieutenant, Levy had turned down a personal offer from Brazil's Emperor, Dom Pedro II, to command a sixty-gun frigate. "I would rather serve as a cabin boy in the United States Navy," he said, "than be admiral in any other service in the world."

Thousands of Jews, North and South, fought and served in the Civil War. Perhaps the most prominent on either side was Judah P. Benjamin. At different times, he was Attorney General, Secretary of War and Secretary of State in the Confederacy. After the war, Jews continued to move westward. Mayor Moses Alexander of Chillicothe, Missouri, went on to Idaho, where he created a small chain of stores in and around Boise.

As governor of the state from 1914 to 1918, he sponsored Idaho's first workmen's compensation law. In Colorado, where the Guggenheim family wrested a fortune from the silver and copper mines, another Jew, Abraham Jacobs, became mayor of Central City, when this boom town was probably the richest and toughest square mile on earth.

Meanwhile, on the Atlantic Coast, Jewish immigrants began to arrive by the tens of thousands, adding a new dimension to Jewish life in America.

Most of the first Jews to reach the colonies had been Sephardim, descendants of Spanish and Portuguese families who, before 1492, had developed a high civilization among the Moors of Iberia and North Africa. By the beginning of the eighteenth century, the Sephardim had been joined by the Ashkenazim. First to come were the Jews of Germany. Then, during the latter part of the nineteenth century, the Jews of Eastern Europe arrived in multitudes.

Under the lash of pogroms in Russia, restrictions in Rumania and poverty in Austria, more than 1,700,000 Jews sought a new life in the United States between 1882 and 1914. They were almost entirely Yiddish-speaking Ashkenazim. They were desperately poor, reaching America with an average of nine dollars. Most of them became workers, particularly in the garment industry in New York. They lived on the lower East Side, which at its peak housed 1,562,000 Jews.

The arrival of such a large group of "strange" immigrants led to considerable antagonism and coincided with another form of discrimination. Descendants of earlier American settlers, having reached wealth and position, were beginning to organize a social upper crust for the first time. This industrial "high society" seemed to need somebody to exclude. The Jews were an historic and, therefore, a ready-made target. For the first time in American history, socially-based anti-Semitism appeared. In 1877, Joseph Seligman, New York banker, was refused admission to Saratoga's Grand Union Hotel simply because he was Jewish. Anti-Jewish exclusion spread through Protestant "society," its clubs and residential districts. By the early twenties, colleges (particularly the professional schools) and corporation offices imposed quota systems against Jews, which have been disappearing only in recent years. At the same time, however, individual Jews were gaining national recognition. Oscar S. Straus became Theodore Roosevelt's Secretary of Commerce and Labor, first Jew to hold Cabinet rank. Louis D. Brandeis in 1916 became the first Jew to serve on the United States Supreme Court.

In the ghettos of New York and elsewhere, the new American Jew began his struggle upward, using education as his chief means of progress. There is an old Jewish saying that a father will "bend the sky" to give his sons an education. Study is part of the Jewish tradition. A Talmudic maxim states that the Jew who is studying the Torah at time for prayers need not interrupt his work to pray, since he is already doing a religious exercise. In America, the emphasis for many Eastern European Jews became the achievement of a college education as the quickest road to economic opportunity.

Thousands of immigrants lived in cold-water tenements, but sent their children to college. In 1908, 8.5 per cent of the male enrollment in 77 prominent United States colleges was made up of first- and second-generation Jews, although Jews comprised only about two per cent of the population. In pharmacy, 18 per cent of the students were Jewish; in law, 13 per cent. Studies of Jewish education in New York in 1948 and 1953 showed that one-sixth of all Jews over 18 had completed college, compared with one-twentieth of the non-Jewish population of the city. In smaller communities, the proportion is believed to have been even higher.

The results of this educational effort have been sensational. By 1916, the Jewish population on New York's lower East Side had melted to only 353,000, and by 1930, to 121,000, reflecting the mobility of an educated people. In Chicago, the ghetto area lost half its Jews between 1914 and 1920. Everywhere, Jews improved their occupational status. Recent studies in 14 cities in which 10 per cent of the Jewish population live showed that from 75 to 96 per cent of Jews were in "nonmanual" work, compared with 38 per cent of the total United States labor force.

Jews are active in all the professions, arts and sciences; they have accumulated six Nobel Prizes and many other awards. They have had a profound effect on American life: in law, Brandeis, Louis Marshall, Benjamin Cardozo and Felix Frankfurter; in medicine, Béla Schick, Selman Waksman and Jonas Salk; in physics, J. Robert Oppenheimer, Isidore Rabi and Edward Teller; in government, Herbert H. Lehman, Anna

Rosenberg, David Lilienthal and Henry Morgenthau, Jr. These are only a few names picked at random from a long list.

Jews also have a long tradition in the American labor movement. Samuel Gompers, British-born cigar maker, founded the American Federation of Labor and was its president for thirty-seven years. Sidney Hillman, late head of the CIO Political Action Committee, and David Dubinsky, president of the International Ladies' Garment Workers Union, were products of Jewish unions in New York City. These unions arose in protest against the old sweatshops, low pay and long hours in the garment industry. Their leaders and many members were dedicated Socialists, but their concern for human betterment never lost its Jewish roots. By the mid-1930's, socialism had begun to decline as a potent factor in Jewish life. When Abraham Cahan's New York *Forward,* Yiddish Socialist daily newspaper, supported Franklin D. Roosevelt in 1936, Jewish socialism, it was said, had become simple liberalism. The New Deal had provided a new concept of social justice.

The Jews' concern for human betterment also has found expression in the less tumultuous area of philanthropy. If any one impulse is commonly characteristic of all Jews in the United States, it is devotion to charity. As a result, the catalogue of Jewish welfare is endless. The American Red Cross was organized in the Washington, D. C., home of Adolphus S. Solomons. Julius Rosenwald of Chicago established a $30,000,000 fund for Negro welfare and education as part of his lifetime contribution of $70,000,000 to charity.

The three Straus brothers of New York, Isidor, Nathan and Oscar, were almost as generous. They built hospitals and tuberculosis sanitariums and even helped found a Roman Catholic church. Nathan set up stations that dispensed 1,135,000 meals during the depression winter of 1914-15, and led the fight for pasteurization of New York City's milk supply. With relatives by marriage in the Lavanburg and Guggenheim families, the Strauses established several huge philanthropic foundations. The Guggenheims themselves set up a foundation, which since 1925 has given educational fellowships to thousands of artists, writers, scholars and scientists.

Hundreds of institutions for human welfare, scattered over the nation, are Jewish in creation and support, although the bulk of the beneficiaries are non-Jewish. In its early days, the Henry Street Settlement in New York was a world model for creative social work and was the cradle of the Visiting Nurse Service. It was founded by Lillian D. Wald and financed by Jacob H. Schiff.

The Federation of Jewish Philanthropies of New York raised nearly one-third of the more than $60,-000,000 spent in 1957 by 116 health and welfare agencies in New York City. In the 12 years from 1946 to 1957, Jewish federations and welfare funds raised $1,600,000,000 for charity at home and abroad. An extra $42,000,000 was raised by other Jewish organizations. This was in addition to contributions to local community chests and other organizations. Many contributions are traditionally made by children in religious schools, where a sense of charity is instilled at an early age.

The community-chest idea itself was conceived by the Boston Jewish Federation in 1895 and was adapted to local fund raising eighteen years later. Another Jewish innovation is the Council of Jewish Federations and Welfare Funds, an association of community organizations. The Council co-ordinates the many national and international appeals, such as the energetic United Jewish Appeal for overseas aid, and analyzes the needs and finances of each.

Jewish women are especially vigorous in welfare and civic work, both locally and nationally; 300,000 are members of congregation sisterhood groups organized for charitable activities. Another 110,000 belong to the National Council of Jewish Women, which sponsors many community services in health, education and welfare.

The most influential Jewish women's organization is Hadassah, a complex of 315,000 members, which is a combined women's club, league of women voters, social-work sponsor and supporter of Israel. It is most active on behalf of health projects in Israel. In America, Hadassah works in the field of adult Jewish education and American affairs. Through nationwide courses, lectures and study groups, these women have played an important role in reviving interest in Jewish culture.

Hadassah reflects the intense interest of many American Jews in the cause of Zionism, the movement for the restoration and preservation of a Jewish nation—Israel —in Palestine. Its roots are planted deeply in religious tradition. For centuries, every Jew has prayed for the return of his people to the land of Abraham. The mod-

ern Zionist movement began about 1862 with Moses
Hess in Germany. It expanded under the leadership of
Theodor Herzl and Leo Pinsker. Herzl's *The Jewish
State,* published in 1896, appeared one year before the
first world Zionist Congress was held in Basel, Switzerland.

Zionism in America always has been controversial,
but the sting of Nazi persecution gave urgency to the
cause and won many adherents whose interest in it was
simply humanitarian. Despite the immense aid to Israel
by American Jews, both in the formative years and in
the years that Israel has been a nation, there is still
some difference of opinion on Zionism. The movement,
having accomplished its primary purpose—the existence
of Israel—has lost both its passionate militancy and its
partisan antagonisms.

Today, Israel excites most United States Jews for
what it may become, and for what it may contribute to
the total Jewish culture. Hadassah's president, Dr.
Miriam Freund, envisions Israel as the fountainhead of
Jewish culture and religion, to which American Jews
can make great contributions without disturbing their
primary identity as Americans, and from which they can
draw spiritual strength. Other Jews here are less san-
guine; they wish Israel well, but expect it to develop a
national existence independent of American Jewish
relations.

In spite of differences, American supporters of the
new state sold $285,000,000 worth of Israeli bonds
between 1951 and 1957. In 1958, 36 per cent of
Israel's foreign exchange came from the United States,

including grants from the Federal Government as well as private loans, contributions and bond sales.

Such seemingly secular aspects of the story of the Jews in America in reality reflect an act of religious faith. Christians can translate the faithful into precise statistics of baptism and confirmation, and gauge piety by acceptance of creeds and church attendance. None of these indexes applies to Judaism.

Jews are expected, though not compelled, to attend synagogue, but prayer itself is a requirement. They do not stress creed. They do not believe in hell and damnation. They do not need to be "saved," in the Christian sense of the word, since in Judaism there is no doctrine of "original sin" for which all men must atone. There is no word in Hebrew for "salvation," in terms of redemption.

Jews are under disciplines, but have no sacraments. God's covenant with Abraham in Genesis was an agreement that He would protect and bless the Jewish people if they remained faithful to Him. It applied not only to Abraham's family, but also to all generations unborn. (God, Jews believe, will protect and bless *all* men who are faithful to Him.) Every Jew comes under the covenant—"The joyous responsibility"—at birth.

Judaism is a way of enriching life, not a doctrine. Like the unwritten British Constitution, some of its vital tenets are assumed, and thus are subject to reinterpretation by rabbinical scholars to meet new conditions.

Basically, a Jew believes that life is good, the gift of God, which man should enjoy, as a creature made in the image of God. At the same time, the Jew is obli-

gated to do what he can to make life happier for everyone—to do justly, love mercy and walk humbly with
God.

Judaism's religious practices consist of an observance
of rituals, ceremonies and customs, many of which center
in the home and commemorate great historical events.
Jewish history is, and always has been, inseparable from
the Jewish faith.

Millions of United States Jews in the past sixty years
have devoted themselves to social and political idealism.
But the new generation, now becoming parents, is dis-
covering that social progress is not enough. The young
people who are third-generation American Jews feel
secure in their acceptance as Americans and are now
seeking a more positive Jewish identity. This requires
synagogue membership, both for the education of their
children and for joint action with other Jews.

Synagogue membership increased between 1945 and
1958 from about a third of the Jewish population to
over one-half. This upsurge has been felt by all three
major Jewish groups—the Orthodox, the Conservative
and the Reform—each of which estimates a million or
more members today. These groups have one fundamental belief in common. All three agree that Judaism
is governed by laws found in the Bible and the Talmud.
But they differ in their opinions on the interpretation of
the laws, as well as on the principle of divine revelation.

The Orthodox Jews in the United States conceive of
a continuous Judaic tradition based upon a divinely
revealed Bible. They regard the observance of rituals

and ceremonies as basic to the values of Judaism. They recite their prayers in Hebrew, they have no instrumental music in their services, and women are seated in separate pews. They keep kosher homes and strictly follow the dietary laws even when away from home. They allow no work of any kind to be done on the Sabbath (the period from sundown Friday to after dark Saturday), not even turning on a light or driving a car.

The concepts of Conservative and Reform Judaism in America developed mainly in the nineteenth century. In 1824, there was a Reform congregation in Charleston, South Carolina. By 1875, under the leadership of Rabbi Isaac Mayer Wise, Reform reached great popularity, and its seminary, Hebrew Union College, was established in Cincinnati.

The Reform Jews believe in principles, more than in practices, and hold only the moral law, or those portions of the Bible relating to ethical behavior, to be divinely revealed. Among Reform Jews, most men no longer wear hats or skullcaps at worship, families sit together, and choirs sing with organ accompaniment. Services are mostly in English. Hebrew portions are translated. The observance of dietary law is not required.

Conservative Judaism developed later than Reform and was partially a reaction to it. The Jewish Theological Seminary (Conservative) was founded in 1887 by Rabbi Sabato Morais. It was not until 1902, however, when the great Jewish scholar Solomon Schechter became head of the seminary, that Conservatism began its rapid growth.

Conservative Jews believe that the divinely revealed Bible is subject to modern interpretations, and that the observance of rituals and ceremonies is a form of character education prescribed by God. More important than the observance itself is its effect on the individual's personality. Thus, Conservative Jewish practices vary widely. In such matters as English in the service, family pews and instrumental music, adjustments are made by individual congregations.

Coincidentally, about the time of the establishment of the Jewish Theological Seminary, the Orthodox seminary, Yeshiva Etz Chayim, was founded. It was the forerunner of Yeshiva University, which includes the major United States Orthodox seminary. Both Yeshiva and the Jewish Theological Seminary are in New York City. Historically, Conservatism and Orthodoxy have had their greatest influence in large metropolitan centers. Reform has been strongest in the South and West, where there are few large Jewish communities.

Regardless of group, Jews as a whole support the Synagogue Council of America, which is a clearinghouse in areas where the entire religious community may want to take united action or require a single spokesman. They readily co-operate within such organizations as B'nai B'rith and its civil-rights arm, the Anti-Defamation League; the National Jewish Welfare Board, which not only represents 353 Jewish community centers but also serves chaplains in the armed forces; and the American Jewish Committee and American Jewish Congress, both of which are energetic champions of civil liberties.

Today, in almost every new suburb where there are a hundred or more Jewish families, a new synagogue is rising, both as a house of worship and as a center for social and religious life. Many of the members have

had little or no contact with a synagogue since childhood, but now they insist that their children be firmly
introduced to their Jewish heritage and to the Hebrew
language.

Religious-school attendance illustrates the awakened
interest in Jewish identity. The day-school movement,
for example, is 60 years old, but until the end of World
War II, it was insignificant. Since 1948, enrollment in
these schools, which teach religious and academic sub-
jects through the twelfth grade, has leaped 64 per cent,
to 30,268 students in 250 schools. Many other youngsters study after public school and on Sundays for a
total of eight hours weekly. Nearly 500,000 children
attend these supplementary schools today, compared
with 239,000 only nine years ago.

Thus, Judaism today is robust and looks to the future
with confidence. It is generating spiritual and creative
energy from which all people will benefit. Its good
health is one sure proof that America's concept of
equality under the law works. From New Amsterdam
to the new suburbia, the Jews have struggled to make
one of the most ancient religious cultures part of the
growth of America's new democratic culture; they have
grown *with* America. Their faith is still being tested
here, not by restriction, but by freedom—not by failure,
but by success.

10

The Seventh-Day Adventists

To a group of slightly more than one million people scattered across the United States and the world, threats of atomic destruction, political chaos, the seemingly general corruption and decay of humanity and the rise of anti-God movements hold no terror. These are the Seventh-day Adventists. For more than a century, the Adventists and their spiritual forebears have anchored their gospel to the conviction that the Advent, the Second Coming of Christ, is imminent and will bring with it man's long-hoped-for perfect world.

The basis of this tenet is an intricate interpretation of the prophecies in Old Testament Daniel and New Testament Revelation, and in the promises of Jesus Himself. To the Adventists, a native American church, these foretell that Christ will return to earth and here establish a paradise for His faithful followers. The event will be preceded by a monstrous war, pestilence and plague, the destruction of wicked humanity and Satan, and the purification of the earth by a holocaust.

Adventist predecessors at one time calculated that Christ's Second Coming would occur on October 22, 1844. It was on that date, Adventists now believe, that the final stage of man's human history began. The hour of Christ's expected return is unknown, but through dedication to His work, Adventists believe they can hasten it. The Bible states that the Advent cannot take place until the Gospel has been preached to all nations. As a result, the Adventists push missionary work with a sense of great urgency. Since their first missionary, John Nevins Andrews, was dispatched to Switzerland in 1874, Adventists have established themselves in 185 of the world's 208 countries. There are at least 40,000 members in the U.S.S.R. and 21,000 in Red China. So zealous are these missionary efforts that occasionally a letter reaches international headquarters in Washington, D.C., addressed to "The Seventh-day Adventurers."

Recently, the Adventist Church crossed the 300,000 mark in United States membership—a 33 per cent growth in 10 years—and it now numbers 1,102,910 followers around the globe. The 41,033 Adventist church workers are astonishingly active. They preach in 748 languages and dialects, circulate $21,000,000 worth of books and tracts each year in 213 languages, broadcast a radio program, "The Voice of Prophecy," heard over a network of 583 United States stations, and a weekly television program seen on 170 stations. They also conduct a Bible correspondence course that has enrolled 3,362,233 students around the world over the past quarter century.

It is not easy to be a Seventh-day Adventist. The Church is scrupulously Biblical. Darwin's theory of evolution is rejected unequivocally. The Ten Commandments are emphasized, not as a means to salvation, but as an expression of the teachings of Christ. The Sabbath, which Adventists observe from sundown Friday to sundown Saturday, is wholly dedicated to the Lord. Adventist shops and factories close, no work is performed, and television and radio are silent.

Adventists may not play cards or dance. They do not smoke, nor do they drink alcoholic beverages or even coffee or tea. They dress simply, avoiding ostentation, and wear only functional jewelry.

Adventists regard seriously the Apostle Paul's teaching that the human body is the temple of the Holy Spirit. Anything that undermines the body is therefore profane. Vegetarianism is widely practiced, on the basis that the Old Testament says man's original diet did not include flesh foods. Adventists also point out that some flesh foods serve as disease carriers when not properly cooked. But they emphasize that they are not living by Biblical legality alone. It is their love and gratitude for Christ the Saviour that makes them want to follow His teachings.

Adventist church work begins with the appeasement of bodily ills. Adventists point out that Christ spent more time healing than preaching. They do likewise. The Church maintains an elaborately equipped College of Medical Evangelists at Loma Linda, California, where medicine, dentistry and nursing are taught in courses approved by the American Medical Association. In the United States and Canada, there are 23 Adventist hospitals and sanitariums, plus two clinics. In other countries, 90 Adventist hospitals and sanitariums and 82 mission dispensaries and clinics treat about 2,300,000 patients each year.

American Adventists are scattered from coast to coast. A 1949 survey shows that three times more Adventists are college graduates than is the case with the general United States public. More of them are married and fewer of them are widowed or separated than census figures reveal for the public generally. Few are wealthy. Adventists tend to be physicians, medical technicians, preachers, managers of small businesses, factory foremen, clerical workers, salesmen, laborers and skilled craftsmen. They have small families, with two or three children the norm.

In religious attitude, Adventists are dedicated and dignified, often more intellectual than emotional. They frown on noisy exuberance in religious meetings as haughtily as do Episcopalians.

The Biblical prophecy that Christ would someday return to earth has always intrigued the Christian world. Since Hippolytus, a bishop of Rome, published his systematic commentary on the Book of Daniel in A.D. 217, an entire literature has grown up around the meanings of the prophetic visions in Daniel and Revelation. By 1836, there were at least 60 dissertations based on the theory that the Advent would take place 2,300 years after 457 B.C.

One of these predictions was written by William Miller, a farmer and justice of the peace in upstate New York. Thus began one of the strangest passages in United States religious history, one that was to have a profound effect on the course of the Seventh-day Adventist Church.

Miller turned to Scriptural study around 1816. For some years, he pondered the prophecies and concluded that Christ would return about 1843 or 1844. In 1831, he began to speak publicly of his convictions. In 1833, the Baptist Church gave him license to preach. He published a sixty-four-page tract and a series of sixteen lectures on the Second Coming. His theory caught fire. Clergymen of various denominations—Baptists, Presbyterians, Methodists and others—listened to his ideas. Crowds attended his lectures.

In 1840, a Boston preacher, Joshua V. Himes, embraced Miller's ideas and gave them showmanship. Himes was a man of action. He established a Millerite newspaper to spread the message. It was called *Signs of the Times,* and later became the *Advent Herald.* Securing one of the largest tents seen in America up to that time, Himes took Miller throughout New England, New Jersey and New York. More than seven hundred ministers of many faiths became disciples and carried the word as far as the remote frontier of Kentucky and Ohio.

The cause reached its climax in 1844. Miller first reckoned that the end of the world would occur by March. When it did not, Millerites put it down to a minor error in calculation. Another Millerite saw the end coming on October 22. Miller was reluctant to be specific in terms of less than a year, but he finally accepted that date.

As the day grew near, many of the faithful, who numbered between fifty thousand and one hundred thousand, sold or gave away their possessions to make gifts to the poor or support the cause, and prepared joyously for the imminent end of the world.

Because some of the founders of the Seventh-day Adventist Church were Millerites, the Church has been haunted by this unfulfilled prophecy.

An Adventist editor, Francis D. Nichol, and a team of researchers a few years ago carefully examined newspapers and library manuscripts of the period for evidence of Millerite hysteria; they found none.

What happened, according to Nichol's findings, was that on the great day, the Millerites gathered in their meeting places and homes to pray and meditate and to await the Second Advent of Christ.

After midnight of October 22, 1844, the Millerites faced the taunts of the public and their own bitter disillusionment.

But the day after the great disappointment, on October 23, 1844, Hiram Edson, an active leader of the movement, saw, as in a vision, what was to become the accepted explanation. He saw, "distinctly and clearly," that October 22 was not the end but the beginning of the end. The Adventists, Edson believed, had misinterpreted the date of Christ's Second Coming. The first 2,300-year prophetic period was at an end, he contended; the final stage of prophecy was just beginning.

There were a few others who refused to be shaken in their belief. In New Bedford, Massachusetts, faith remained in Joseph Bates, a retired sea captain turned abolitionist and temperance advocate. Bates was an Adventist. He wrote a pamphlet urging Christians to adopt a belief held by some Baptists and return to a Biblical Sabbath, observing the day of rest from sundown Friday to sundown Saturday.

In Maine, there were two others who refused to be disillusioned. They were James White of Palmyra, a preacher in the Christian Church, and his fiancée, Ellen Gould Harmon of Portland. They were married in 1846.

With Bates and a few others, they were to become key-stones of the Seventh-day Adventist movement.

What renewed Pastor White's zeal was a vision experienced by his fiancée only two months after the Miller prophecy had failed. While kneeling in prayer with friends at a family altar in south Portland, Ellen became transfixed. She entered into her first vision. In this state, she saw the bedraggled Adventists as part of the faithful "remnant" of Christians prophesied in Revelation. In a second vision, experienced shortly after the first, she was shown the trials through which she would pass, and was told it was her duty to relate to others what had been shown to her.

Today, the Seventh-day Adventists believe that they, with other faithful Christians, will form the "remnant" people when Jesus Christ appears again on earth.

Ellen White had her first vision in December, 1844. Subsequently, she had many more. Although her husband was cautious about revealing them, lest the ridiculed Adventists be the victims of further derision, they found their way into print. The visions encouraged the straggling Adventists, who now began to come together in twos and tens. Meanwhile, Captain Bates's "Sabbath keepers" were swelling the slowly growing Adventist movement.

Ellen White never claimed to be a "prophet." She saw herself as a "messenger" through whom were relayed God's desires and admonitions. (Seventh-day Adventists believe that her visions give clear evidence of their divine inspiration.)

The work of the early organizers was disappointingly slow. To make a living, White cut stone, labored as a farm hand and split cordwood. After 1850, he edited the Adventist newspaper, *Review and Herald,* which stemmed partially from *The Present Truth,* the first Seventh-day Adventist publication, founded in 1849. But the newspaper, rather than his family, ate up most of his earnings.

At first, Adventists simply met in informal "bands." The first church of what was to become the Seventh-day denomination was not organized until 1855, when John Byington, a Methodist minister, led his flock of fifty at Buck's Bridge, New York, into the Sabbath keepers' fold. The same year, Captain Bates, who had migrated to Michigan, helped to build a church in Battle Creek.

On the frontier, Adventism found a warm welcome. James and Ellen White visited Battle Creek in 1853 and then moved the Adventist newspaper into a two-story frame building in Battle Creek in 1855. On a hill overlooking the Kalamazoo River, a tabernacle was built. Eleven years later, a medical institution was started, and eight years after that, a college. In 1863, with a membership of 3,500, a national conference of Sabbath keepers organized as a denomination—the present Seventh-day Adventist Church. Some Adventists opposed the move. They argued that such an organization would solidify them and put a label on them.

During these formative years and until her death in 1915, Mrs. White was the acknowledged inspiration of the movement, though the administration remained in the hands of many men. Her writings were accepted by Adventists as having been produced under divine guidance. They were not viewed as supplements to the Bible, but merely as guides to doctrine in many fields. From her visions and admonitions, which embrace 53 volumes, 4,500 articles and great quantities of personal letters, Adventists received their direction. So great was Mrs. White's literary output that, in her books alone, she wrote 6,000,000 words. She probably wrote another 19,-000,000 words in her articles. Her ideas established the mold of Adventism in its medical, educational and missionary work around the world.

When she was in a vision, Ellen White was formidable. Her husband in 1868 gave what is probably the most comprehensive description. She was utterly unconscious of everything around her, he said, and viewed herself as being removed from this world and surrounded by heavenly beings.

Sometimes, in a trancelike condition, she appeared to suspend her breathing for a period of from fifteen minutes to three hours. Her muscles became rigid, and her joints were fixed. On coming out of a vision, of which she had between one hundred and two hundred, her power of sight did not return for about three hours. Her visions came on her anywhere: as she preached, while praying or in her home. Ellen White was accused of suffering from everything from epilepsy to schizophrenia, but no doctor was ever able to make any such diagnosis stick.

Because many Adventists were not organization-minded, the movement remained a fairly haphazard one until the turn of the century. By 1903, membership had grown from 3,500 to 75,000. There were 20 publishing houses turning out 80 periodicals in a dozen languages

and other publications in 30 more languages. The movement had 126 health institutions, and Adventist secondary and college-level schools numbered 35, with
several hundred elementary church schools. There were
900 ordained ministers, and the church treasury was
administering over $600,000 each year. All this growing
plant was laxly run, a situation that was to become critical in the case of the denomination's most celebrated
individual, Dr. John Harvey Kellogg.

John Harvey Kellogg, the father of corn flakes, was
one of sixteen children of an early Michigan Adventist.
He was to publicize Adventist health principles the world
over.

Dr. Kellogg was encouraged by Mrs. White to study
medicine so that the Adventist beliefs of "health reform"
might be soundly grounded medically. The Adventists
believed in sunlight, fresh air, a simple diet and discipline
against overindulgence. Mrs. White and Dr. Kellogg
were advanced in their medical ideas. She gave early
voice to the influence of the mind over the body's well-
being, and advocated such activities, daring for that day,
as hydrotherapy and physical therapy.

Evidence of the effectiveness of Adventist health
theories was recently reported by the Sloan-Kettering
Institution. A study of Adventists revealed that they
suffer substantially less than the general public from
cancer and heart disease.

In 1866, the Adventists had opened the Western
Health Reform Institute in Battle Creek. Dr. Kellogg
became its director in 1876. He changed the name to
the Battle Creek Sanitarium.

Kellogg's idea was to add to the advantages of a normal hospital all the recently developed resources of physiological medicine, plus scientific diets and nutrition. The aim was to stress the principle of curing through natural methods—proper rest, exercise, mental hygiene and simple foods. The unique character of the "San" was recognized by doctors around the world, and patients flocked to it.

Dr. Kellogg became aware that the meatless diet at the "San"—every menu listed the units of protein, fat and carbohydrates in each dish—was monotonous. Some illustrious patients even sneaked across the street to a shanty restaurant called the Red Onion for an occasional illegal steak.

Kellogg began to experiment with tasty meat substitutes. In the course of his search, he invented corn flakes, peanut butter and a hundred other health foods. Kellogg's indefatigable crusading for public health made the entire nation diet-conscious. Dry breakfast cereals became a national staple. Fresh fruit and vegetable salads appeared on the nation's tables in place of heavier fare.

In 1907, after bitter countercharges, Kellogg was expelled from the Adventist Church over three major areas of disagreement: control of the sanitarium, management policies at the institution and theological variance. Kellogg took the "San" away from the Church.

Shortly before this time, the Church undertook to reorganize itself. A system much like Methodism was set up with a general conference at its head, and regional and local conferences to direct day-to-day activities. A change of the location of national headquarters to a more centrally placed city had been discussed earlier, but Adventist roots were deep in Battle Creek. Here were the Adventists' chief publishing house, their college and academy, their general offices and, before the expulsion of Dr. Kellogg, their sanitarium.

What some took to be the hand of God now intervened. A series of fires ravaged much of their property and opened the eyes of the faithful. The Church found land in the Takoma Park section of Washington, D.C., and in 1903, headquarters were officially transferred. The move proved auspicious. When Mrs. White died in 1915, membership had grown to 140,000, and the clergy had increased to 2,500. There were now 40 publishing houses scattered around the world, and 80 medical institutions. The Adventist educational system had burgeoned to 5,000 Sabbath schools, 700 day schools and 70 advanced academies and colleges. There were Adventist missions on each continent.

Along with the move came a reorganization of the financial structure designed to consolidate finances in a central system administered by the General Conference. The new system permitted prosperous churches to transfer funds to more needy areas. This had two results: It inspired members to give more to their church per capita than the followers of any other religious group. It also gave the Adventists a fiscal policy unique among Protestant denominations.

One out of every nineteen Adventists works full time for his church. These employees—foreign missionaries, doctors and nurses, pastors, teachers and executives—all receive almost identical pay and living allowances adjusted only to take care of differences in local costs of living, age and experience. The pastor of the big headquarters church in Takoma Park could be paid the same as the leader of a flock of fifty in the Ozark Mountains. The same pension and health benefits apply to all. The present world president of the General Conference of Seventh-day Adventists, Reuben R. Figuhr, a Wisconsin-born former missionary who speaks fluent Spanish, German and Tagalog, draws $89.50 a week. All other church workers, even college presidents, receive slightly less.

Adventist officials, as a result, have little money to spend idly. They tell the story of a Midwestern church conference that disappointed local merchants and restaurateurs. When the Adventists left town, the Chamber of Commerce secretary said glumly, "They came to town with the Ten Commandments in one hand and a ten-dollar bill in the other. In a week's time, they didn't break either."

The per capita contribution of United States Adventists to their church as reported in 1957 was $212.80, compared with an average of $56.74 for 41 other Protestant and Eastern Orthodox churches reporting income in the same year. The bulk of the Adventist income is from a tithe, which Seventh-day members pay scrupulously. This voluntary ten per cent of each member's income finds its way to a central fund, from which international expenses and all salaries are paid. Money for local expenses of individual churches is raised in addition to the tithe. There are weekly offerings—for radio and TV work, missions, temperance education, publications and schools.

Ingenious methods are used to increase Adventist collections. Many churches, for example, have a "seed-money" project. Sabbath-school members invest a small sum in a project (raising and selling flower seeds, for example), and contribute the profit for the Lord's work. Sewing circles make and sell rag dolls. A Colorado Adventist offers uranium rock to tourists from a road-side stand. A California woman breeds goldfish. Teen-age teams glean fields at harvesttime and act as baby sitters. Youngsters collect bottles for the deposit. By such methods, Seventh-day Adventists in 1956 amassed $510,000 to swell missionary funds. Occasionally, the fund-raisers get carried away. In a California church, the women rented a store for a rummage sale. Business was so brisk that one of the ladies sold the rug off the floor—only to discover later that the rug belonged to the store.

While the casual observer might gain the impression that Adventists tend to be a bit eager in their money raising, activities of this sort are actually part of a program outlined by the Church.

Such eagerness is engendered at an early age. Recently, on a Los Angeles television station, a seven-year-old panelist revealed that his father was an Adventist minister. Asked what distinguished his church, he replied, "Ours is noisier than the others." What he meant was not that the Adventists whoop it up with old-time spiritual fervor (they don't), but that there is sometimes considerable commotion in Adventist meetings. This is because even the tiniest babies are expected to be in church on Saturday morning, though they will not become members until they are in their early teens.

Hence, in churches without special "cry" rooms, there is often an overtone of infant sobs and parental talk, and considerable travel to the rest rooms. Adventists develop the churchgoing habit early.

Adventist preachers—many are called "elder," but the trend is toward the title "pastor"—speak calmly over the juvenile sound effects. They are actually teachers more than preachers. Many Adventists take their Bibles to worship service and turn to each text as it is mentioned. Since the Adventists are Biblical literalists, every statement made by the preacher must have sound Biblical documentation. A pastor may cite as many as ten different texts during a half-hour discourse. Ellen White, in her sermons, set this precedent. She once quoted fifty texts.

The Seventh-day Adventist liturgy is much like that of the Methodist Church, except that no creed is recited. The service is on Saturday rather than Sunday. And the Adventists are probably the only Christian denomination that prints in its weekly bulletin the time of sundown on the following Friday and Saturday, marking the beginning and end of the Sabbath. Adventists usually address each other as "brother" and "sister."

Six out of every ten Adventist youths, at each level of education from elementary school to college, are educated in the Church's own schools. Adventists are firm believers in parochial education as a means of instructing their young in Seventh-day views on Scripture and health.

Adventist young people, of whom there are currently about 62,000 in United States, and Canadian Adventist schools, apparently do not chafe under a doctrine that includes Saturday Sabbath, a meatless diet, simplicity in dress and the discouragement of most commercial entertainments. Adventist home and school environment is such that young people are indoctrinated early. Their beliefs are an integral part of their upbringing.

In their loyalty to the Church, Adventist young people reflect the dedication typical of most older members. Boys and girls appreciate the oft-told story of the missionary in India who was asked, "If you weren't an Adventist, what would you be?" The missionary replied unhesitatingly, "I would be ashamed of myself."

Since the Second Coming will be preceded by natural upheavals and war, the Church has an extensive disaster-relief program, which is also motivated by the Christian desire to respond to human needs. More than any other church, it works with Civil Defense in preparation for catastrophe. The Church conducts its own first-aid training program, which is rated one of the best by the American Red Cross. Each parish has a Health and Welfare Society and a Civil Defense Committee. In these agencies, 23,500 people have received Red Cross first-aid certificates since 1950. Some Adventist state organizations have caches of relief supplies and trucks to transport them. Many of these vehicles are painted with the Civil Defense symbol.

The Church has developed a "survival" kit and a "disaster" kit which many Adventists carry in their cars. During the Civil Defense alert at Washington, D. C., in 1954, thirty-three Adventists—the youngest six weeks old, the oldest sixty years—camped out in bitter cold for three days in order to test the survival kit under severe conditions. The survival kit weighs twelve pounds. It provides a high-calorie, high-protein diet for three days from powdered milk, dried fruits and eggs, pre-cooked oatmeal, twelve ounces of sterile water and other items. The disaster kit has water-purification tablets, medicine and bandages.

In any disaster, the Adventists are well organized. In the tornado that hit Worcester, Massachusetts, in 1953, the woman president of the Health and Welfare Federation for Southern New England was prepared to act swiftly. By prearrangement, she had a telephone priority with which she mobilized members from thirty-seven churches at the Adventist welfare center at North-boro. First aid was given to scores of tornado victims. By nightfall, canteens were feeding the homeless. For ten days, the Adventists fed from five hundred to seven hundred people daily and distributed ten thousand pieces of clothing.

Similar mercy mobilizations were made during the 1955 floods in Connecticut and in 1957, when tornadoes took a heavy toll in the South.

Mercy is also emphasized in Adventist military service. Adventist men are classified 1-A-O under the draft. They are eligible for duty, but only in noncombat jobs. Adventists are assigned to medical or other non-combat units by directive of all the armed services. Under local camp arrangements, church members are usually excused from Sabbath duty and stand watch on Sunday instead. The Church's schools have their own equivalent to ROTC in their Medical Cadet Corps. The

MCC trains more than fifteen hundred draft-age boys a year for medical-aide duty—a project approved by the United States Army's surgeon general. One product of this program, Corporal Desmond T. Doss of Rising Fawn, Georgia, won the Congressional Medal of Honor on Okinawa during World War II.

The Adventist philosophy of Christianity is summed up in a brochure for prospective students at the College of Medical Evangelists. The school's purpose, it says, is "to guide in the development of a balanced sense of values as revealed in intellectual, ethical and spiritual attitudes, to engender and nurture the desire to give selfless service to mankind."

In practice, this ideal is epitomized by a charity patient who one day entered an Adventist hospital on the West Coast. After treatment, he seemed reluctant to leave without saying something. A doctor encouraged him to speak.

"I'm just trying to figure you out," the patient said. "I've been treated by many doctors, but here I'm puzzled."

"How so?" the physician asked.

"Well," the patient said, "your medicines are the same—but the touch of your hands is different."

11

The Disciples of Christ

ETWEEN THE APPALACHIAN MOUNTAINS and the
Pacific stand some eight thousand churches whose
members reject any denominational label. Many
simply call themselves "Christians," believing that since
Christ founded their religion, His name alone should be
used to describe His followers.

These people have one great aim: to consolidate all
Christians into a single fellowship based on the simple,
straightforward teachings Jesus gave to His Disciples.
They would free Christianity from the contradictory
doctrines and disciplines that men have superimposed
on the religion in the past two thousand years.

The Christian Churches have developed from several
roots, but now most of them are loosely united through
an organization named the "International Convention of
Christian Churches (Disciples of Christ)." Today, these
Christians—or Disciples, as some prefer to be known—
number nearly 2,000,000 in America and more than
320,000 in 17 other countries. This makes them seventh
in size among United States Protestant communions.
They are the largest religious group that had its origins
on American soil.

From 1950 to 1957, the Disciples added 78,000 new
members who were previously affiliated with another

denomination or with no church whatever. The reason
for this growth is that the Disciple approach is liberal,
intellectual and independent. I talked to a woman who
joined a Christian church because, having lost her newly
born baby before it could be baptized, she was told by
her minister in another group that the infant had gone
to hell. This she could not believe. I found several
women who had enrolled because they could not accept
the instruction of another faith that religious duty obliged
them to bear children, though all of them were mothers
of three or more youngsters. A man told me he had a
fundamental block from the doctrine taught him in
childhood that all human beings are basically sinful and
must spend their lives in atonement. Another man left
a church from which a bishop had arbitrarily removed
the pastor against the desires of the congregation.

All these people found spiritual comfort among the
Disciples, who embrace no creed and have no official
doctrines. The Christian Churches reject any organization that would have power to tell them what to do or
think. Their ordinances (they do not call them sacraments) are limited to the two described in the New
Testament: baptism of believers by immersion and the
fellowship of all Christians through a symbolic Lord's
Supper. In many Christian Churches, members do not
refer to their minister as "Reverend," since he has no
special powers they do not possess.

The Disciples have discovered that many persons
cannot stand up on Sunday and espouse the Apostles'—
or some other—Creed, yet devoutly desire to be Christians. For many of them, the virgin birth, a literal heaven

and hell, the ultimate physical rising from the dead, a last judgment of all human beings and other doctrinal points are personally unacceptable.

The Disciples sweep away all conflict on such issues. They say, "Believe what you will, after studying your Bible. The acceptance or rejection of dogmatic principles cannot keep any sincere person from reaching God or Christ." Thus the Disciple fellowship ranges from those who hold every syllable of the Bible to be the literal word of God, to humanists for whom the Bible is inspirational only. Being Christians, however, all avow Jesus Christ as the Son of God. Almost all concede that the soul has some form of immortality, but its exact nature is a question that each believer must decide for himself.

Disciple principles have been epitomized in four great slogans:

No creed but Christ, no book but the Bible, no name but the Divine.

Where the Scriptures speak, we speak; where the Scriptures are silent, we are silent.

In essentials, unity; in opinion, liberty; in all things, charity.

We are not the only Christians, but Christians only.

These slogans do not imply, however, that the Christian Churches are a catchall for unbelievers or for ethical culturists who uphold the moral values of religious disciplines without the obligations of Christianity. Far from it. The Disciples are intensely New Testament-centered. Freedom to decide does not, to the

Disciple, release him from the obligation to search the Scriptures and learn what God expects him to do.

It is true that the Disciple is released from any categorical position on such social questions as drinking, birth control or divorce. But the New Testament establishes definite obligations on all followers of Jesus, and these obligations the Disciple must weigh and abide by, according to his own conscience and intelligence.

The idea of designating followers of Jesus simply as "Christians" without denominational status was probably first used in America by James O'Kelly. In 1792, he led a small group away from the Methodist Church in Virginia and North Carolina. The group reached a strength of more than twenty thousand and ultimately was absorbed by either the Disciples or the Congregationalists.

About 1801, two New Englanders, Elias Smith and Abner Jones, broke from the Baptists. By 1807, their group included fourteen churches, also known as "Christian," which emphasized the right of all believers to think for themselves. In 1808, Smith began publication of the *Herald of Gospel Liberty,* probably the first religious newspaper in America. The views of this paper had great influence on the Disciple movement. Many overtures to consolidate the two groups failed, however, and the New Englanders ultimately merged in 1931 with the Congregationalists to form the Congregational-Christian Churches.

A frontier Presbyterian minister named Barton W. Stone was deeply influenced by O'Kelly. Born in Maryland in 1772, the descendant of a colonial governor,

Stone was reared in southern Virginia by his widowed mother. He attended a Presbyterian academy, but early showed a dislike for the rigidity of his church's doctrine. Stone was a revival-meeting preacher who, with more zeal than theology, persuaded the rustic backwoodsmen to accept conversion.

The intellectual Presbyterians could not condone this. They placed two other revivalists on trial. These revivalists resigned from their synod, along with Stone and two others, and formed what they called the Springfield Presbytery. But only a few months later, in 1804, Stone and his colleagues wrote a satiric *Last Will and Testament* over the body of the new organization. This document is one of the cornerstones of today's Disciple movement.

In this Testament, they repudiated denominationalism and all creeds that divide Christians. They urged followers of the Bible to unite in a new order, based solely on the Scriptures. Stone and his associates adopted the name "Christian" for this movement, and their arguments won an instant hearing on the frontier. At that time, preachers of a dozen denominations, all claiming they had an exclusive ladder to heaven, had so confused the settlers that many did not know what to believe. The Presbyterians, in particular, were swept into Stone's orbit, depleting that denomination in parts of Ohio and Kentucky. By 1827, the Stoneites numbered 12,940, from Kentucky and Tennessee to Missouri.

By a different route, a father and son, as intellectual as Stone was instinctive, were reaching Stone's theological conclusions. They were the Campbells: Thomas, the father and thinker; Alexander, the organizer and builder, one of the greatest debaters ever to emerge on the American continent.

Thomas Campbell, a Scot who lived in northern Ireland, was a schoolmaster and preacher. With seven children to feed, he sought a land of richer opportunity. In 1807, at the age of forty-four, he migrated to America, leaving his family to follow later. By good fortune, he reached Philadelphia while the Presbyterian Associate Synod of North America was in session. Immediately, he was accepted as a preacher and sent to southwestern Pennsylvania. Less than six months later, he was in trouble, accused by fellow pastors of heretical teaching. Withdrawing from the church, Campbell became a freelance preacher and organized a society in Washington, Pennsylvania, called the Christian Association of Washington. This was not a new denomination, but merely a discussion group of fellow intellectuals. Brooding over his treatment by the Presbyterians, Campbell began to write a statement of his religious beliefs. He had just completed this *Declaration and Address,* now considered the Magna Carta of the Disciple movement, when, in 1809, his family arrived.

The oldest child was Alexander, twenty-one. He had been carefully tutored in his father's school, but dissent was in his blood. While studying at the University of Glasgow after his father's departure for the New World, Alexander was closely questioned by church elders on the articles of Scottish Presbyterian faith before being given a small metal token permitting him to take communion. He answered the questions, then scornfully flung the token in the church plate and stalked away. After that, he rejected all man-made creeds as conditions for reaching God. On his arrival in America, he and his father found themselves, much to their surprise, in almost complete theological agreement.

No one has ever expressed the cause of nondenominationalism more cogently than the elder Campbell. The *Declaration and Address,* a pamphlet of fifty-six pages, called for the unity of all Christians in independent local congregations. These would throw off all man-made religious notions and go back to the Bible as the sole authority for faith and practice. Campbell did not argue for the creation of a new church, but for the merger and purification of existing denominations, sects and factions.

After Alexander's first child was born in 1812, he and his father decided that infant baptism was not Biblical and that adult immersion was mandatory in the New Testament. Alexander was immersed by a Baptist preacher in a creek, together with his wife, father,

Here was a cause that young Alexander could espouse with enthusiasm. He began to preach and soon drew a modest following in what is now West Virginia. The Christian Association became the Brush Run Church. About this time, young Alexander married, an event that indirectly had great impact on the Disciple movement. His bride was the daughter of a wealthy farmer and millwright. Four years later, Alexander was deeded his father-in-law's prosperous farm. This made him independently wealthy. He never afterward accepted a penny for preaching, establishing a tradition, which died hard, that Disciple ministers should receive no salary and should not stay with one congregation.

mother and a sister. With this step, a theological requirement was nailed into the Disciple movement, baptism of believers by immersion. The Campbells and their church were accepted soon after into the Redstone Baptist Association. They remained "reformers" within the Baptist Church until 1830, when they withdrew and became known as "Disciples of Christ."

Gradually, Alexander became the leader of the movement, and his father receded into the background. For twenty-five years, however, the elder Campbell traveled widely on the frontier, particularly in Kentucky, Virginia and North Carolina, preaching and organizing. So intense were his labors that he was away from home for nine months of every year for nearly a decade, as he regretted in a letter he wrote his daughter when his wife died at seventy-one. From his eightieth birthday until his own death at ninety, he traveled little, content to be the patriarch of a growing flock.

Most of the early Disciple preachers were itinerants, ranging the backwoods in search of converts. They were rugged, dedicated zealots. William Hayden, who canvassed Ohio and detoured into New York, Canada and Michigan, practically lived on horseback for twenty-five years. Many Disciples were farmers who felt the call to preach, and left their farms to do so in the winter months.

There were few church buildings. Meetings were held in the open or in schoolhouses, barns or private dwellings. As churches were erected, they were extremely simple, without steeple, bell gallery, altar, pulpit or lectern. And, of course, there were no organs, since such music was unscriptural. Having few permanent preachers, the laymen themselves conducted the services and administered the Lord's Supper, except when an evangelist happened by.

Settled preachers remained rare until the second half of the nineteenth century. The evangelists heralded their coming in many ways. Walter Scott, leader of the Disciple movement in Ohio, was the most spectacular. He would engage children in debate and send them home to tell their parents he would preach that night.

Another colorful crusader was John Smith, a Tennesseean called "Raccoon John." He became a Baptist preacher at twenty-three. Eager to work in the Alabama wilderness, he moved there with his wife and two children in 1814 and built a log cabin for his family. His new home burned, destroying both children. The shock of the accident killed his wife and shook Smith's theology. In 1824, he became convinced of Campbell's cause and started a career as a tart-tongued traveling evangelist.

At Owingsville, Kentucky, Smith once chanced on a Methodist meeting as the preacher was about to baptize a child by sprinkling water on the infant's head. This rankled the Disciple as a believer in adult immersion. As the minister prayed with his eyes closed, Smith slipped to the altar and drank the baptismal water. When the prayer ended, Smith chortled, "Brother, I drank your Jordan dry."

Raccoon John's greatest achievement was his role in the merger of between twelve thousand and twenty thousand Disciples with ten thousand Kentucky "Christians." Barton W. Stone, the Christian leader, had long advocated such a union. On January 1, 1832, both

Stone and Raccoon John were in Lexington, Kentucky, when the groups were merged.

By 1840, Alexander Campbell had become a frontier celebrity. That year, he founded Bethany College, now in West Virginia. His magazine, *The Millennial Harbinger,* was widely read. He had been a member of the Virginia Constitutional Convention. James Madison called him "the ablest and most original expounder of Scripture I ever heard."

Campbell had also edited, amid great controversy, the first United States attempt to translate the New Testament into modern English. This venture sold more than forty thousand copies and in many respects anticipated, in translation and scholarship, the Revised Standard Version of the Bible.

Wherever he went, crowds gathered at road toll stations, ferry slips and other places where he had to stop, while celebrated local preachers challenged him to theological debate. He was delighted to oblige. His friend, the Roman Catholic Archbishop of Cincinnati, John B. Purcell, said that Campbell's impromptu arguments demolished his opponents by such pungent logic that the debates rarely lasted very long.

The Archbishop had good reason to know of Campbell's powers, for he met him in one of five debates Campbell had with religious figures. The debates made Campbell world-famous and drew so many converts to the Disciples that a national convention was formed.

By now, Campbell was at the height of his powers, a tall, gaunt man with a great mop of hair, a hawk nose and blue-gray eyes under opulent lashes. His lung power was formidable. When he spoke on the thirteenth chapter of I Corinthians, "faith, hope and charity," he allotted an hour to each of the three. A college president who knew him wrote, "His conversations were declamations, but all were willing that they should be so."

A debate Campbell had in 1837 with Purcell, then bishop, on Roman Catholic claims so won Purcell's admiration that they remained life-long friends. Campbell climaxed his debating career in 1843 against a famous Presbyterian preacher, N. L. Rice of Paris, Kentucky, with Henry Clay as moderator. Their main subject was baptism, and they disputed for 16 days. Each would speak for an hour, and then each would rebut for alternate half-hours until a particular point was exhausted. Then the routine would begin all over again. Each made 64 speeches, taking time off on Sundays. A transcript of the debate that was sold throughout the world ran to 912 pages.

By 1849, the movement numbered more than 118,000, held together by common interest and by the personalities of Campbell, Scott and a few others. (Stone had died in 1844.) Some adherents called themselves Christians and some Disciples.

The Civil War caused no rupture. Not being a denomination, the Disciples took no position in the conflict. A few years later, however, they were torn by debate over whether instrumental music and missionary societies were Biblical. On these two issues, the difference of opinion became so intense that the conservatives, who made up about half the membership, drifted away and consolidated in 1906 as the Churches of Christ. This group today claims to be as large as the Disciples, with two million members.

One Indiana faction took the Bible so literally that, since organ music was not mentioned in the Bible and could not be used in churches, it deliberately built a new church with doors and windows so small that the liberals could not install an organ. In St. Louis, members purchased a building that already contained an organ, but a majority voted against its use. The minority seceded and set up in a rented hall that had no organ. Thus the anti-organists had an instrument and would not use it, while the pro-organ faction wanted one and had none.

The view on missions was equally stubborn. Both liberals and conservatives interpreted the Bible as obliging all Christians to go "into all the world" and preach the Gospel. However, conservatives argued that if Christ had wanted a missionary society, He would have formed one. The first general convention had set up a voluntary mechanism called the American Christian Missionary Society, but it received little support. In 1874, the women of the church formed a Christian Woman's Board of Missions, sent missionaries to Jamaica and India and began work at home. By 1900, most of the opponents of the missionary societies had withdrawn from the Church, and in 1920, the United Christian Missionary Society was established. Thus, the Disciples had definitely committed their fellowship to a vigorous, organized missionary policy.

The Disciples remained primarily a rural church until recent years. They established themselves in large numbers in the West. For two decades, they were the strongest religious group in Oregon. Between 1900 and 1945, a 52 per cent increase in membership gave them more than 1,700,000 members. But they attracted almost no immigrants, being content to recruit among what they called "Old Americans."

On social questions, lacking united power to act, they have had minor influence. An agency reporting to the International Convention now has departments that represent the movement on social-welfare problems, race relations and social justice. Individual conduct is still a purely personal matter with each member.

In 1953, a Disciple study found that, because of enormous shifts of population, sixty-seven per cent of the Disciples lived in towns and cities, whereas sixty-five per cent of their church buildings were in rural areas. The city churches grew while many of the crossroad assemblies withered. Of the total affiliated congregations, seventy-four per cent were in the Midwest, South and Southwest. The survey showed also that individual Disciples had made economic progress and were rapidly climbing into the middle and professional classes.

The International Convention, handicapped by a lack of denominational authority, created an executive staff in 1946 to promote activities on which all Disciples could agree. This headquarters is in Indianapolis. Other national agencies are in St. Louis and Nashville. These are denominational in organization, although some members won't admit it. National agencies operate a pension fund, guide missionary activity in eleven foreign fields, act as co-ordinators for most church boards and commissions at home, and lately have become aggressive in expanding the number of churches.

The international organization is financed by such voluntary contributions as local churches care to give. A plan called "Unified Promotion" is now in effect in about half the affiliates and budgets stated sums for 56 activities. But only voluntary contributions support the 20 Disciple colleges, six theological seminaries, 17 homes for the aging or for children and 30 regional philanthropic agencies. Disciples gave their churches more than $78 million last year, an average of $47.77 per member, low among Protestant groups. Of this, 86 per cent was spent locally.

The Disciples emphasize their role as leaders in the movement to unify all Christians, and members of the Disciples have been in the front rank of all interchurch movements. They helped to organize what is now the World Council of Churches. In 1959, there were 209 Disciples on boards and commissions of the National Council. This participation makes the Disciples, with the Presbyterians, the strongest source of interchurch man power. On the local level, the Disciples are equally vigorous. Their pastors are diligent in community affairs and in county and state inter-denominational work. For 100 years, Disciples have talked merger with the Baptists, and for 25 years, with the Congregationalists.

But they are pulled in two directions at once. "We are in a peculiar position," says the Disciple executive secretary, Dr. Gaines M. Cook. "We would like to in-

crease our effectiveness by organizing as a denomination to get things done. But if we do, we risk adopting
positions that other churches cannot accept, thus jeop-
ardizing the cause of union. We do not dare to crystal-
lize, or we lose one of our chief causes of being, which
is to be ready at all times to merge with other Christian
groups."

Despite this tug of war, the Disciples move ahead.
They have added more than 200,000 members since
1955. They propose an intensive campaign between
1960 and 1970 to establish two new congregations a
week and increase their financial contributions by 50
per cent.

"We will do it, too," Dr. Cook says. "Denominational lines are breaking down. Everywhere, more people
are giving their loyalty to Christian living rather than
to denominational dogmas."

12

The Mormons

THE MORMONS—literally, the members of the Church of Jesus Christ of Latter-day Saints—have never been understood by their fellow Americans. Every year, a million tourists visit the Mormons in Salt Lake City, Utah. They enter a tabernacle so acoustically responsive that the drop of a pin at the pulpit may be heard in the eight-thousandth seat. They may hear a recital on one of the world's great organs or an anthem by one of the finest choirs to be found anywhere. Outside the city, they marvel at the irrigated farms planted in a barren desert.

But never are visitors permitted inside the high-roofed Temple dominating Temple Square. It is a prohibition pointing up a salient fact about the Church: Mormonism is not just a creed; it is a complete way of life.

The early history of the Mormons is a saga of tragic and sometimes bloody misunderstanding. They were driven by violence from Ohio to Missouri and then to Illinois. In desperation, they trekked finally from an unfriendly United States to the Great Basin of the Rockies, only to find the region annexed to American territory within a year. Persecuted with the passionate hatred often roused by new or "different" religions, harassed by the militias of two states and a United States infantry expedition, pilloried for their practice of polygamy, they none the less survived and today are exceedingly vigorous. There are 1,416,731 of them in the Utah-centered Church alone, plus more than 160,000 in other branches. An excommunicated group, which numbers perhaps 400 devotees, still practices polygamy in secret.

Mormons are different.

They will uproot themselves from home, family and prosperous careers to become missionaries or nonpaid religious administrators. They will undertake any other assigned task anywhere in the world at the call of their leaders, and consider this sacrifice a privilege. To keep their bodies healthy, they are told not to use alcohol, tobacco or even coffee or tea. Worthy Mormons wear a ceremonial undergarment. Officially, the Church opposes birth control, but the members want large families anyway. Every male is expected to be ordained to the priesthood at the age of twelve, and nine out of ten of them are. A few Negroes have become Mormons, but they can't be ordained to the priesthood.

The Church provides for its faithful like a mother hen. It has no professional clergy, but, largely through volunteers, it manages one of the most amazing religious-social-economic organizations in history. Mormonism is a self-reliant society, which distributes the bounty of all its people to any member in need. Mormons do not believe in Government doles. There is freedom from want in a chain of farms, storehouses and granaries that keep on hand—together with what is stored by each family—enough food and clothing to supply *every* Mormon for a full year. There is complete companionship in a snobless social order, which revolves around the ward hall, a building at once chapel, community center and second home. There are opportunities for education equal to one's aptitude, the development of hobby skills under expert teachers and a job worthy of one's ability.

The religious spark that fires off such community of effort is a belief that God became supreme by mastering universal knowledge, and that everyone on earth is a spiritual son or daughter of God. His children have human form as one stage of their existence, to test them and increase their knowledge. If worthy, in a future life they will resume their bodies and will be exalted in the kingdom of God, which will be built upon the American continent.

Mormons rear large families the better to provide human bodies for these children of God. Because Mormons hope to achieve divinity, it behooves them to live saintly lives on earth. Marriage in a Mormon Temple is the first step toward divinity. Only ten Temples are in use in the world today, the most famous being the Salt Lake City Temple, built by volunteers between 1853 and 1893. These are not churches or chapels for public worship, but the scenes of sacred ceremonies. Only the worthy are permitted to enter and be wed: thus Mormon boys are dedicated to the Church, and Mormon girls are virginal and industrious.

Such a religion, in these modern days, should work better in theory than in practice. But the Utah Mormons

—now spreading rapidly through the Western states and with settlements throughout the world—never get away from it. They are reared in Church-ordered homes and live rather clannishly in close-knit communities that provide all their wants and needs. Under such circumstances, Mormons have difficulty in breaking away or nonconforming, even if they want to. Most Mormons have little desire to relinquish certain divinity for transient self-indulgence. Withdrawals and excommunications average only seven per month, far offset by 24,000 annual conversions and a birth rate of 36.6 per thousand, compared with a national average birth rate of 24.9.

Take the case of John Buehner, a middle-aged, intelligent, soft-spoken Mormon of Salt Lake City. He and five brothers own a building-materials company. But this is merely his bread and butter. His first duty is the Church. He is bishop, or local leader, of East Stratford ward, a tightly integrated eight square blocks under Mormon hegemony. In the ward live 240 Mormon families (only 24 non-Mormon families reside in the area), and the ward hall is the center of their existence. They include salesmen, bank employees, teachers and a few professional people.

Most of the East Stratford families are well educated. None are wealthy. Few Mormons get rich in a religion that inspires pooling of talent and resources for the good of all. The cash contribution commanded by the Church from every Mormon is ten per cent of earnings, plus about two per cent more for the local ward. These are voluntary contributions, and no collection plate is ever passed in a Mormon chapel. But tithing is another criterion of worthiness, so most Mormons pay gladly.

Bishop Buehner knows his flock intimately. He or his representative visits each home once a month and keeps a record of everyone's religious progress, community service and personal need. If a widow's lawn requires mowing, the bishop sends a young priest to the job. If someone is in want, the bishop draws on his abundant storehouse for anything from meat to oven-hot bread, and delivers these stores by truck. In a disaster, he would call on brother bishops for aid. (During the Yuba City, California, flood, on December 26, 1955, the first relief truck to enter the area carried four tons of food and bedding for the 110 Mormon families in need of assistance.)

Whenever someone needs a job, Bishop Buehner finds it, either temporarily in a Church-owned co-operative or permanently among friendly employers. When a parishioner is sick, Buehner sends out a member of the Women's Relief Society or arranges for doctor or hospital, with no questions asked about ability to pay. When members backslide—as even Mormons do—the bishop dispatches representatives to inspire them. He plans parties, picnics, athletic events, receptions, theatricals and music lessons, guides college educations, buries the dead. Nobody in the ward may enter the sacrosanct Temple in downtown Salt Lake City without his written "recommend," which means that tithes are paid up, the person's religion is devout, and his personal conduct is unblemished.

Bishop Buehner spends about forty hours a week in ward work, and receives not a penny for it. He did not ask for the job; it was assigned to him by the Church leaders. He has held his position since 1952 and will stay until released, whenever that may be. In his youth, he was a missionary in Germany for two years, paying his own expenses.

Sunday is unique in Mormonism. It begins at 9:00 A.M. with priesthood meetings attended by all males twelve years old and up. Here, the work of the ward is organized; religious studies follow. The priesthood is graded upward in six degrees, from twelve-year-old deacons through teachers, priests, elders and seventies to high priest, a lofty position attained after years of study and service. From the priesthood are chosen, by the church-at-large, a Council of Twelve Apostles, who constitute a group of ruling elders; from these, by seniority, a Church president is sustained with life tenure. Since April 6, 1951, David O. McKay has been president of the Church. He is more than eighty years old. In Bishop Buehner's ward, there are twenty-seven high priests, but none has ever been chosen an apostle.

In the East Stratford ward—one of 1,947 wards in the Church—the women and children do not arrive on Sunday until the priesthood meetings adjourn at 10:00 A.M. Then there is a meeting for everybody, open to all ages. This is called "Sunday School," but it is not one in the usual sense. It includes a sacrament of bread and water; many members, old and young, participate in the ritual. Girls from ten to sixteen are prominent at Sunday School, reciting two-and-a-half-minute homilies of their own composition. I heard Julia Stagg, sixteen, speak on the necessity for consistent observance of the sacrament, and Lujean Taggart, fifteen, delineate the little sins that in aggregate become big sins. An eleven-year-old, Cheryl Smith, led the sacramental Scripture reading from memory, then stood in the pulpit, her arms folded, while the sacrament was passed.

After a forty-five minute convocation, the meeting breaks up into age-group classes similar to non-Mormon Sunday schools. At 5:00 P.M. on Sunday, there is another sacramental service for adults. Because there is no paid clergy, selected members of the ward give the sermon.

On Tuesday or Wednesday, all the young people assemble in the ward hall for meetings of MIA, or Mutual Improvement Association. These are so universally attended that public-school teachers expect little homework to be accomplished on MIA night. For the boys, there are sports, Boy Scouting and hobby instruction; for the girls, dramatics, music, homemaking and preparation for the role of mother of a maximum family. In MIA, there is opportunity for courtship and friendship, for the organization is a beehive of sociality.

Statistics of the entire Church for 1956 show that MIA activity included such staggering totals as 15,926 dances; 550 dance festivals; 9,728 dramatic presentations involving 66,009 players, plus 799 drama festivals in competition with other wards; debates and orations for 43,846 participants and choruses using 61,149 voices. In sports, there were 4,555 teams and 67,400 players. The all-Church basketball tournament alone drew 25,000 participants, some from overseas.

Sacred Temple ceremonies of the Church are never discussed specifically in ward meetings. They are revealed only in the Temple itself. "Jack Mormons," as some are called, are excluded from these ceremonies. This epithet, from pioneer days, refers to the jackass who brays loudly, but pulls little weight in the traces. For those allowed in, Temple rites are primarily of two types: proxy baptism for the dead and marriage.

A unique feature of Mormonism is that baptism may be performed for the dead, by proxy, as well as for the living. Mormons believe that in the latter days, when Christ will rule the world for a thousand years, families will be resurrected, assume physical but deathless bodies and resume life together. A Mormon's ancestors who died before the religion was revealed to mankind may be baptized by proxy as the first step in their acceptance of the true faith. The Church maintains in Salt Lake City one of the most complete genealogical libraries in the world, in which Mormons may research their ancestry and then, in the Temple, be baptized, by total immersion, for their forebears. Baptism of the living may take place anywhere that there is enough water for total immersion, but proxy baptisms must be performed in the Temple font, which is in a room said to be a duplicate of a hall in the temple of Solomon.

Also in the Temple, couples are "sealed" in marriage, not just for life on this earth, but for "time and all eternity." To the Mormon, marriage lasts forever if properly solemnized in a Temple. In the celestial kingdom to come, the man-wife relationship will be resumed. Persons not "sealed" in a Temple may become angels, but they will be of a lower order, who will be servants to the elect.

Mormonism is unique among religions. Every two weeks, some seventy to ninety young men and women— the boys twenty years old, the girls twenty-three—leave for two years of missionary work. Their modest expenses, averaging $60 a month, are paid by themselves or their parents. What impels them to go? I watched the ceremony that set apart sixty-nine young people for this task, then picked one at random for questioning. He was Bruce Ballard, a handsome, stocky lad from Duarte, California. He had played football at U.C.L.A., including the Rose Bowl game of 1956, and had graduated with a Phi Beta Kappa key. After five months at medical college, he was called by Church leaders to be a missionary. How did he like that?

"I was honored and humbled," he said. "I am thrilled that this is the work God wants me to do. Mormons are the happiest people in the world. I want to help others to find our happiness." His glowing fiancée, who sat beside him, nodded in proud agreement. She will wait for him.

I talked to a returned missionary, Diana Woltjer, a tall blonde with large blue eyes and a soft, almost bashful voice. Although girls cannot hold the priesthood, Diana knocked on doors in northern Holland, making contacts and teaching. She subsisted on fifty dollars a month, sharing a room in a private home with another girl missionary from whom, under Church rules, she could not be separated day or night. What had she accomplished?

"I feel," she said, "that my life has changed greatly. I know now what my religion means, for I have seen the Spirit at work in the mission field. I have seen the Gospel change the lives of people. I will never have a happier two years." Today a private secretary, Diana goes out several evenings a week as a missionary to non-Mormons in Salt Lake City.

The missionary spirit pervades even the famous Tabernacle Choir, directed by Richard P. Condie and known to radio listeners from 29 years of Sunday network broadcasts. The 375 singers rehearse four hours a week and spend an aggregate of $8,000 a year on transportation, though none receives any pay or expenses. They know 800 anthems. Members seldom miss a rehearsal or service. Some commute 75 miles in car pools. Loey Newren, a basso, has not been absent in 12 years. What do they get out of it, beside the thrill of participating in one of the world's great choral groups? "We could sing in our ward choirs with much less effort," one told me. "But in the Tabernacle, we represent the Church. We are missionaries, after a fashion, and that is what we want to be."

I also saw how the Church influences members' lives at a spring prom at Brigham Young University, the big Mormon school—it has 10,000 students. Not a girl was arrayed in an immodest gown. Not a bottle or a cigarette was to be seen anywhere. There was no necking between dances, no rowdyism of any kind. The dance opened with a prayer and closed with a hymn. Everybody had a wonderful time.

Such is the religion Joseph Smith, Jr., revealed and Brigham Young built. Today, it covers the West with sufficient vigor to be a substantial factor in the politics of several states. In Utah, seventy per cent of the people who belong to any church are Mormons, and they have now overflowed their original home to plant large concentrations in Idaho, California, Arizona, Wyoming, Washington, Oregon and, in the East, in Washington, D. C.

The Church is rich. Its pioneer investments in Western land, natural resources, manufacturing and finance have expanded with Western growth, and today are huge. The leaders do not reveal the Church's net worth, though some members of the Council of Twelve Apostles are directors of railroads, utilities and national corporations, representing Church-owned stock. Productive real estate alone totals 978 buildings. The Church budget for 1957 was $57,000,000, not counting about $30,000,000 to pay expenses for the local wards. But even this does not reflect the total effort, for the 5,102 missionaries labor at their own expense, the 372,531 officers and teachers draw no pay, and there is no extensive payroll for any purpose.

The Mormon movement grows rapidly. Six hundred new ward halls are currently under construction; three new chapels have been dedicated each week since 1950. Two new Temples have been built—one in England and one in New Zealand. (Of the ten other Temples now in use, seven are in the United States and one each in Canada, Switzerland and Hawaii.)

Since, in the Mormon belief, achieving divinity involves supreme knowledge, the Church pays unusual attention to education. Utah is not exceeded by any other state in its rate of college graduates, and Mormons claim to have a higher rate of listings in *Who's Who in America* and on the registers of scientific honor societies than people of any other faith.

The list of prominent Mormons is impressive. In government, it includes Secretary of Agriculture Ezra Taft Benson and United States Treasurer Ivy Baker Priest. In science, there are the television pioneer Philo Farnsworth; a chemist, Dr. Henry Eyring, whom the *Saturday Review* has called one of America's ten outstanding scientists, and Dr. Harvey Fletcher, author of fifty-two textbooks on electricity and acoustics. In business, the list includes the financier Marriner S. Eccles; a past president of the United States Junior Chamber of Commerce, E. Lamar Buckner; the president of Standard Oil of California, Theodore S. Petersen; and the president of American Motors, George Romney. Among many prominent artists is Arnold Friberg, a designer of costumes for the Cecil B. DeMille motion picture *The Ten Commandments.* Mormon accent on sports and entertainment has produced a middleweight boxing champion, Gene Fullmer; Miss America of 1952, Colleen Kay Hutchins of Arcadia, California; America's prettiest schoolgirl of 1955, Lorna Young of Salt Lake City; and Miss America of 1957, Charlotte Sheffield, also of Salt Lake City. The "All-American Family" of 1957—Mr. and Mrs. Frederick E. Bergeson and their four children of Shelley, Idaho—are Mormons.

The Church of Jesus Christ of Latter-day Saints is a thoroughly American institution. It emerged during a period of great religious upheaval after the Revolutionary War, when men challenged their Christian tradition as passionately as they had overthrown British authority. The larger denominations, particularly the Methodists, Baptists and Presbyterians, openly competed with one another, until a mighty din of religious controversy reverberated, particularly on the frontier.

Greatly disturbed by this hubbub was a fourteen-year-old boy of scant education and humble parents who lived near Palmyra, New York. His name was Joseph Smith, Jr. He was a handsome, tall, flaxen-haired youngster with intense hazel eyes mellowed by unusually long lashes. He was a strong wrestler, a handy axman, sure in the saddle, an outdoorsman. He had other qualities too—a surprisingly gentle voice and a friendly smile, which disguised a strong streak of stubbornness. With his mother, Joseph attended revival meetings and heard the competing preachers. One day in 1820, having meditated on James 1:5, he went into the woods to decide what to accept from this babel of religious tongues. He had a vision of God the Father and His Son, Jesus Christ, who appeared to him in a shining light and told him not to join any established church, for all of them were distortions of the Way which Christ had founded. Instead, the boy was told, Christ would restore His original precepts, and Joseph Smith would be the instrument of the restoration.

For the next seven years, Joseph awaited instructions. From time to time, he was visited by the Angel Moroni, who, in September, 1827, allowed him to take a box which had been hidden in a hill. This contained golden plates on which were engraved strange hieroglyphics. A pair of "instruments"—called Urim and Thummim—were provided, by means of which Joseph Smith could interpret the text. To a local schoolmaster,

Joseph Smith dictated a translation, after which the plates were returned to the angel. The *Book of Mormon* was published in 1829, and in 1830, a new religious faith was born.

This book, in 300,000 words similar in style to the King James Bible, details the story of two bands of Israelites who settled in America and from whom certain American Indians are descended. Christ visited these peoples after His resurrection, and thus they preserved Christianity in its pure form. The tribes were liquidated in battle about A.D. 385. The last of the race, one Moroni, hid the nation's sacred writings, compiled by Mormon, his father. They remained buried until Moroni, now an angel, disclosed them to Joseph Smith at the command of God.

The Prophet Joseph Smith's original concept was as simple as the Sermon on the Mount. It restored not only Galilean Christianity, but the familiar cast of Biblical characters: saints, prophets and apostles, who banded together to live pure lives and await the second coming of Christ. Its appeal to converts was that it answered every controversy then raging in the Christian world. On the direct revelation of God, the Prophet Joseph Smith could assure his followers that what he said was true. And the faith was sure-footed, containing no such theological dogmas as transubstantiation, impanation, regeneration or justification, which were just so many words to the rustic backwoodsman.

So Joseph Smith took his message to the frontier. In February, 1831, only a year after the organization of his church, he, his bride and a few disciples moved to Kirtland, Ohio, on Lake Erie. By June, 1831, their zealous missionary efforts had brought two thousand converts into the fold.

During the next 13 years, Smith had 135 direct revelations from God that greatly developed his movement. He established at Kirtland a community that grew from 150 to 1,500 in six years. The idea, never fully realized, was that he, a prophet as Moses had been a prophet, in direct communication with God, would rule a community both temporally and spiritually. Another precept was that, at His second coming, Christ would establish in America the land of Zion. Scarcely settled at Kirtland, Joseph Smith went to Missouri on a scouting trip and located the Promised Land in Jackson County. On August 3, 1831, on the highest promontory in the vicinity, 63 acres of holy ground, he dedicated and marked the exact spot on which the Temple of Zion, Christ's earthly headquarters, was to be built. He then returned to Kirtland, and sent newly won converts to live in Jackson County, Missouri, near the present site of Kansas City. By October, 1833, there were 1,200 Mormons on Jackson County farms.

(Today, the Reorganized Church of Jesus Christ of Latter-day Saints has about 10,000 members in Independence, Missouri—more than any other church. This branch of Mormonism was brought together in 1860 under the leadership of Joseph Smith III, son of the Prophet. It now has 159,996 members in 875 congregations in the United States and Canada, and missions abroad. The Reorganized LDS builds no Temples, hence it practices no Temple rites. It always rejected polygamy. Its present leader is a direct descendant of the Prophet, a son of Joseph III named Israel A. Smith.

Still another branch, called the Church of Christ, Temple Lot, actually owns the plot of ground on which Christ's Temple was to be built. This group does not have funds to erect a Temple, and claims it rejected an offer of $5,000,000 from the Utah Mormons for the property. Still, all Mormons today look toward Independence, which will be the capital of the world when Christ returns.)

But trouble beset the Saints. Until 1847, wherever they settled, they were driven out. They regularly voted Church policy in local elections, and it was feared that they would gain political control.

In November, 1833, the Mormons were driven at gun point from Jackson County. They re-established themselves in the northern part of the state, and within five years numbered more than five thousand and controlled five counties, having been joined by the Prophet Joseph Smith and his Ohio following. Under the goading of Missouri's governor, the state militia liquidated the Mormon settlements. At Haun's Mill, for example, a detachment killed seventeen men and dumped their bodies in a well, then scattered the women and children in a forest. After heavy losses, the Saints fled to Illinois.

Within three years, the Mormon town of Nauvoo, with Joseph Smith as mayor, was the largest city in the state. Nauvoo had its own militia and a legislative body with power parallel to that of the state government. It appeared that Smith soon might seek control of Illinois. The Mormons nominated him for President in 1844, and a number of men even campaigned for him.

Meanwhile, in 1842, an apostate Mormon, John C. Bennett, revealed for the first time the practice of polygamy at Nauvoo. From then on, the Mormons were reviled on social as well as political and economic grounds. Added to this was the fierce jealousy of the non-Mormons, who envied the successes of Mormonism in and about Nauvoo.

Bitterness against them became so intense that Governor Thomas Ford of Illinois summoned the militia to Nauvoo on June 10, 1844. The non-Mormon public had been inflamed after Mayor Joseph Smith had forcibly suppressed an anti-Smith newspaper, the Nauvoo *Expositor*, published by dissident Mormons. The paper's publisher tried to have the mayor arrested. The Prophet avoided arrest, but now the non-Mormon element demanded a trial.

Joseph Smith was summoned by the governor to the county seat in Carthage, Illinois, was arrested, released on bond and arrested again, this time for, of all things, treason. Governor Ford ordered the Prophet placed in the Carthage jail for his own safety and assigned two companies of militia to protect him.

On June 27, 1844, a mob of 150 men with blackened faces stormed the jail and murdered Joseph Smith. The militia had not saved him; indeed, there is strong evidence that the militia itself participated in the martyrdom of the Prophet.

Leadership of the group passed to a glazier and painter from Vermont, forty-three-year-old Brigham Young, who had led the exodus from Missouri.

Brigham Young intended to remain in Nauvoo. But public animosity was unrelenting. Under pressure, Young announced that, in the spring of 1846, he would lead his people to a land "so unpromising that nobody will covet it." He found such a place in Utah. On July 24, 1847, leading an advance force of 143 men and three women in 72 prairie schooners, Brigham Young looked into Great Salt Lake Basin.

He knew from the explorations of John C. Frémont, four years earlier, that this 27,000-square-mile area, with its salted lake and no outlet to the sea, was no paradise. The land belonged to Mexico, not to the United States. Here, if anywhere, was earth nobody wanted. Said Young, "This is the place!" By nightfall, Elder William Carter had plowed a half acre, and Elder Wilford Woodruff had planted a sack of potatoes. The Saints had found haven at last.

The 30 years from 1847 to 1877 qualify Brigham Young for the distinction of being one of the great colonizers of all time. In one year, 450 houses were built for a population of 5,000. One hundred twenty babies were born. Then, with 5,000 acres of grain awaiting the reaper, a scourge of crickets descended. The settlers, whose lives depended on their food, fought the pestilence with water, fire and shovel, to no avail. They then resorted to prayer. Moments later, a flock of sea gulls winged from the west and began to feed on the crickets, and did not depart until the disaster was averted.

A few facts from Brigham Young's colonizing effort give some idea of his genius. He planted identical towns on streams, about ten miles apart, all with wide streets and disciplined construction. All rodent-inviting barns were placed outside the villages. Each settlement was a Church colony, from which residents spread out to work adjacent farms.

Within 10 years, the Mormons had built 135 communities with a population of 76,335, flung as far away as Idaho, Wyoming, New Mexico and California. By 1877, when Brigham Young died, there were 360 towns with 140,000 people.

Leader Young aimed to make his colony self-supporting, right down to artificial flowers for the dining table, and in 10 years, the job was done. A revolving fund to finance immigration attracted 85,220 new Mormons. Many were people of some substance who gave up everything to come to Zion. Many more were hand-skilled converts from the distress caused by the industrial revolution in Europe; these were chiefly British and Scandinavians. So tough and dedicated were the immigrants that between 1856 and 1860 no fewer than 4,075 European converts, determined to reach Zion or die, actually pushed handcarts from the railway terminus at Iowa City, Iowa, to the Salt Lake Valley, a distance of 1,300 miles.

Over every detail, Brigham Young presided. He was churchman, governor and nursemaid to a surging flock. A courtly, polite man, he sat each morning in his office and addressed himself to the new problems of a frontier society. Nothing was too imaginative or too pedestrian to engross him. He promoted a telegraph company, a railroad and an elaborate system of co-operative manufactories with retail outlets.

"He slept," says a chronicler, "with one eye open and one foot out of bed." He was canny. "I do a lot of guessing," he said in a sermon, "and most of the time I guess right." He was an American "original" and deserves the title of greatness.

Brigham Young emphasized play as well as work, culture hand in hand with drudgery. He created the finest theater in the West and the biggest tabernacle, and began the famous Salt Lake City Temple, for which four yoke of oxen required four days to drag one granite foundation stone from the hills to the site. He imported dance instructors, musicians and schoolmasters. He organized orchestras, choruses and debating societies. Nobody hesitated to approach him, even on trivial matters. One day, a woman complained that her husband had told her to go to hell. "Well," Brigham Young answered gently, "don't go."

All this empire building was unknown to the American public, which was being propagandized against the Mormons due to their practice of polygamy. Actually, the extent of this phase of Mormonism was highly exaggerated. Limited to responsible Church leaders, it never exceeded three per cent of the Mormon population at any time. Stern rules concerning it were enforced. Some remarkable families resulted from the practice of polygamy. The biggest descendant family of polygamous Mormonism is that of an obscure English convert, Elder John Tanner, whose blood kin on Mormon genealogical rolls today number five thousand.

Utah became a United States possession by the Treaty of Guadalupe Hidalgo, which ended the Mexican War in 1848, just nine months after the Mormon colonization of Salt Lake Valley. The Mormons organized the "state" of Deseret and sought admission to the Union in 1849. A United States territory, with Young as governor, was set up in 1851, but it was largely Church-directed, with local bishops acting as magistrates.

The Church and its policies became an issue in the presidential election campaign of 1856. A year later, there was a report that the Utah territory planned to secede from the Union. The United States Government sent General Albert Sidney Johnston, with 2,500 troops, to depose Brigham Young's governorship. Johnston's forces remained 40 miles away for three years, while Young negotiated, cannily surrendering the titular governorship, but retaining practical control through the Church. In 1861, Johnston's forces withdrew; they were needed for the Civil War. The conflict was not resolved until 1887, when Federal law disenfranchised Mormon voters and seized all Church properties. But by then, Prophet Young, the great colonizer, was dead, and a second generation sought peace and statehood.

The Church had grown far beyond its isolated valley, its membership numbering eighty-seven per cent of Utah and forty-three per cent of Idaho. (Today forty per cent of all Mormons live in Utah, twelve per cent in California, eleven per cent in Idaho.) Faced with extermination, Church leaders capitulated. Without surrendering belief in the eternal principle of celestial marriage, they discontinued the teaching and practice of polygamy in a manifesto ratified in October, 1890. Statehood, with restoration of Church property and voting rights, followed in 1896.

In the past sixty-two years, Mormonism has flourished. At times, its members have been labeled a "strange people," but they are not strange. They are different, yes, but the right to be different is the essence of the American dream. Whenever assimilation could be squared with the fundamental tenets of their faith, the followers of Joseph Smith and Brigham Young have assimilated.

In keeping with other minority religious groups, the Mormons want to be accepted. The Church has even established an office to help it in maintaining good public relations. But more solidly than most minorities, the Mormons have insisted on their right to pursue happiness in their own way.

This they have done, and it has, indeed, made them happy.

13

The Christian Scientists

To the CHRISTIAN SCIENTIST, pain, sickness, unhappiness and business reverses can be wiped out by a scientific understanding of God. So can sin, all discord and even death. This happy state of affairs is no remote "up yonder," to be entered in an afterlife. The individual may begin to demonstrate it here and now.

Christian Science teaches that everything commonly called material substance is an illusion. An infinite mind, otherwise called God, and His universe of spiritual ideas are the only realities. To the Scientist, God is perfect; He can create only perfection. Therefore, anything that is less than perfect is not of God and consequently does not really exist. Belief in evil is destroyed by knowing the truth. The result is ideal harmony, peace and love.

Obviously, with the proper application of Science, no one should be ill, deformed, unsuccessful in career or marriage or affected by war or hurricane. If the ideal is not achieved, the fault lies not in the divine science. It is due to imperfect application of Principle, just as a mathematician, through miscalculation, may get the wrong answer to a problem. Only Jesus Christ has demonstrated the Principle perfectly, Scientists concede. But today, it is claimed by Christian Scientists, the sick are healed even of cancer and tuberculosis, the polio-crippled child walks, the broken neck knits, physical ugliness vanishes. The farmer escapes drought, wards off hailstorms from his young wheat, keeps his flocks healthy. The businessman, scientist and worker tap undreamed resources to solve their problems. Vice is overcome; character is changed; new purpose and significance enter the individual's life. The Christian Science Church has many thousands of documented case histories attesting that these things have been done.

This emphasis on individual spiritual effort has compelled Christian Science, one of the world's youngest denominations, to develop a new approach to the ministry. There are no preachers and no missionaries. Followers are attracted to the religion by healings, or by the appeal of the idea that good alone is real. Mastery of Christian Science is achieved solely by prayer, study and close association with God, who is described in seven synonyms as immortal Mind, Spirit, Soul, Life, Truth, Love and Principle. Thus, the religion is intensely personal, requiring little or no gregarious activity. As a result, the church has no women's guilds, men's societies, youth fellowships, not even a choir, and it holds no church suppers or social hours. The church property is maintained exclusively for purposes of worship and study; not even weddings or funerals are held within its portals.

In place of activities, Christian Science supports a unique program. The Sunday service highlights readings from the Bible and from the Christian Science textbook. On Wednesday evening, members gather to testify publicly how their lives have been changed through application of divine Principle. Every church sponsors a reading room, which is open daily for study of church-supplied literature. Sunday school, only for youths under the age of twenty, is scholarly; there are no crayons, chalkboards or visual aids, even for the toddlers. Affiliated with every congregation is at least one Christian Science practitioner, who helps individual Scientists, and interested non-Scientists, find and apply the Truth in their own lives.

Since earliest times, mankind has been intrigued with the idea of divine healing—an aspect of metaphysics, or that which is beyond human forces. Where Christian Science departs from other metaphysical systems is in its insistence that God's harmony in the universe is scientific. This claim was made by Mary Baker Eddy, the founder of the Christian Science movement. She maintained that, as in mathematics, adding two and two must always produce four, so metaphysical law, properly interpreted, must achieve a predictable result. Thus, the Scientist sees nothing miraculous in God's curative works. The cure results from a scientific understanding of God and the faithful application of His law. The law works not only in physical healing, but can—and eventually must—cure all the disorders the world is heir to: war, famine, pestilence, jealousy, hatred, death.

Mary Baker Eddy was born in Bow, New Hampshire, on July 16, 1821, the youngest of six children in the family of Mark Baker, a prominent farmer, Congregational deacon and justice of the peace. A frail child, she received most of her education at home under the tutelage of an older brother, who was a brilliant student at Dartmouth College. In 1843, at the age of twenty-two, she married a young man of Concord, New Hampshire, named George W. Glover, who had a contracting business in South Carolina. After only a few months of marriage, Glover died of yellow fever. After his death, his wife bore a son. She returned to her father's house, so chronically ill that her child was taken from her and adopted by his nursemaid.

Mrs. Eddy sought aid from many sources to alleviate her frailness: from medical men, faith healers and spiritualists. She undoubtedly was familiar with the metaphysics of such philosophers as Hegel, Kant, Fichte and Berkeley, and for a time was the patient of a healer named Phineas P. Quimby in Portland, Maine. Little by little, her experience and studies crystallized into a science of the mind that was to go beyond any previous metaphysical thinking.

In 1866, aged forty-four, while living in Swampscott, Massachusetts, Mrs. Eddy slipped on an icy sidewalk in nearby Lynn. She was then Mrs. Daniel Patterson, unhappily married to a dentist, from whom she was divorced in 1873. Mrs. Eddy was severely injured in the fall. In her bed, she read the ninth chapter of Matthew, wherein a man sick of palsy is ordered by Jesus to take up his bed and walk. Pondering this passage, she concluded that life is not composed of material substance, and that God, the spiritual power that controls the universe, is incapable of evil and therefore could not be responsible for disease. She got up, cured of her injuries and of the malady that had plagued her all her life.

Now, she was convinced that God operated through changeless law. Re-reading her Bible with this in mind, she saw new significance in many passages. She studied the subject for three years and began writings she believed to be God-inspired. To prove scientific cause and effect, she brought about several cures: of a teamster run over by a heavy wagon, of a thirteen-year-old girl suffering from tuberculosis, of a cripple with useless arms, of an insane man who invaded her house. These demonstrations convinced her that she had discovered a great truth. She began to teach. In 1875, she published the first edition of her textbook *Science and Health,* to which in 1883 she added a Bible commentary, *Key to the Scriptures.*

Her teachings spread slowly. Mrs. Eddy attracted a few students who began to assemble on Sunday to hear her talk. One of these, Asa Gilbert Eddy, a Boston sewing-machine salesman, she married in 1877. Eddy became the first Christian Science healer to call himself a Christian Science practitioner; he died in 1882.

Mrs. Eddy had no thought of organizing a separate denomination, but hoped to work within the established Christian churches. All early meetings of Scientists were held on Sunday afternoons, so that they would not conflict with the services of organized faiths. But in 1879, the Church of Christ, Scientist, was chartered under Massachusetts law, to protect Mrs. Eddy's doctrine from the contamination of imitators. And two years later, she founded the Massachusetts Metaphysical College, in which she taught Science to four thousand students before disbanding the institution in 1889. Both moves were effective. By 1888, scores of imitators, including some former students, had set up about thirty competing schools and about twenty publications. But by then, there were practitioners and teachers in New York, Philadelphia and Chicago, as well as in Massachusetts, and the circulation of the *Christian Science Journal* was four thousand.

The healings of Christian Science rapidly increased the membership during the next decade, in the face of ridicule from sensational newspapers, lampoons by such noted writers as Mark Twain and the persistent objection of organized medical societies which sought to prevent practitioners from following their profession. By 1895, Mrs. Eddy's adherents had built the Mother Church in Boston, and Mrs. Eddy had written the *Manual of the Mother Church,* containing bylaws under which the denomination operates—without the slightest deviation—to this day. Since 1910, when Mrs. Eddy passed on, these bylaws have been administered by a church Board of Directors. The board numbers five persons, who are self-perpetuating in that vacancies are filled by people chosen by the surviving members, not by election.

At Mrs. Eddy's passing, December 3, 1910, there were 1,114 Christian Science branches of the Mother Church in the United States and 133 abroad. By 1958, these had expanded to 2,416 branches in the United States and 750 abroad. The 1936 United States Census, the last to publish religious affiliation, listed a United States Christian Science membership of 268,915, of whom about 31 per cent were men. There has been some growth since then, for between 1936 and 1958 the church has expanded by 289 new United States congregations, of unannounced size but probably averaging about 100 members. Eighty per cent of the world's Scientists dwell in the United States.

How Christian Science works in the life of an ordinary community is best illustrated by example. York, Pennsylvania, is a brisk city of about 63,000 persons, not far from Gettysburg. Twice a week, and occasionally for business meetings, the Christian Scientists of York County gather in a colonial-type brick church. They number about 140, with another 60, all under age 20, in the Sunday school. On an average Sunday morning, most will be there, and none will be late. They will come prepared, having studied all week the readings prescribed by the church-at-large for emphasis at every Science service that day. Almost without exception, York Scientists, on rising every morning, read from Scripture and Mrs. Eddy's textbook and meditate and pray for perhaps an hour. This turns their thoughts to God, they say, brings them inner peace, instills in them brotherly love and fortifies them with confidence to master any problem the day may bring.

Having no human pastors, Scientists acknowledge the Bible and the textbook as their preachers. The Sunday service is principally comprised of readings from these two sources. A first reader presides and articulates passages from Mrs. Eddy's book, and a second reader, a woman, cites from the Bible. In lieu of a choir, there is a vocal solo by a paid singer. There are three hymns, sung standing by the congregation. Prayer is silent, followed by repetition of the Lord's Prayer aloud, into which, after each phrase, the first reader injects an interpretation of the prayer by Mrs. Eddy. The entire service lasts less than an hour.

On Wednesday evening, about half the congregation assembles for a meeting at which members may testify. The night I was there, the narrations were all of physical healings. A woman said her child had been bitten by a venomous snake; prayer caused the initial angry swelling to subside overnight. A bedridden cripple, despairing of help from medicine, sought aid from Science through a practitioner and had led a normal life for two years with no recurrence of the malady. A retired Army colonel recounted an experience in Korea in which he and another Scientist, by applying Principle at long range, had cured a Korean woman of cholera. A man testified to complete cure from the enslavement of alcoholism. All these testimonies were spontaneous.

Few members of the York congregation are second-generation Scientists. Most have been drawn in by a healing. Having despaired of relief through medical skills, they say, they have been cured by Christian Science.

The *Christian Science Journal* lists six practitioners in York. These are all students of Science sufficiently advanced in training and perception to make a career of helping less assured members live by their faith. Like doctors, practitioners charge for their services, and have no other occupation. In York, their fees are about the same as those levied by doctors for an office call.

One of these practitioners is Mrs. Sophia M. Reist. She has been a practitioner since 1922. Mrs. Reist does most of her work at home. Two-thirds of her patients seldom see her professionally; they telephone, she talks to them, then prays about their problem. In Science, the healer need not see the patient. Science recognizes no limitations of space and time. These are man-made, hence do not really exist. The dynamic, in absent treatment, is not a thought transfer, but a spiritual co-operation between practitioner and patient by which both bring the Truth to bear on an error of thought that has caused an imperfection to develop. The disturbance may be an emotion—anxiety or fear; it may take the form of sickness, even acute or malignant illness.

In her thirty-six years of practice, Mrs. Reist says she has had ample demonstration of the effectiveness of Christian Science healing. She recently worked three days, around the clock, to prevent a suicide; the patient has recovered. Called to a home where a ten-week-old baby had a dangling, useless leg, she reminded herself that the innocent cannot suffer; she discerned that the illness stemmed from parental discord and helped the parents to rediscover each other. The baby, Mrs. Reist says, was cured.

In an apparently malignant case, Mrs. Reist claims similar success. Two doctors, after X-rays, had advised a woman to have a lung removed. Frightened, the patient decided to try Christian Science. The practitioner refused to listen to the diagnosis, saying the nature of the ailment was unimportant. Instead, she helped the patient to a point of view which dispelled her bitter resentment that "God" would cause her such suffering. Mrs. Reist explained that God had nothing to do with it, that it was not in accord with His will, and sent her home to study Science. Several weeks later, X-rays disclosed no trace of the former condition.

On an individual level, Scientists direct their daily lives according to their understanding of Principle. In moments of doubt, or a crisis beyond their own skill, they call a practitioner for help, and also search the Bible or their textbook and other writings by Mrs. Eddy for help.

A member of the York church, and a teacher in the Sunday School, is Carroll Boyd. He is a clean-cut, clear-eyed, neat young man just turned forty, father of a college-sophomore daughter and a son graduated from high school. One Christian Science tenet is that man creates his own hell on earth. Carroll Boyd believes this. He has been through hell, and says Christian Science led him out of it.

Boyd was in World War II. Afterward, he could not settle down. He became an alcoholic. In his deranged state, he was disconcerting to his family. He could not hold a job. A psychiatrist told Mrs. Boyd her husband was no good, and recommended that she leave home and start a new life for herself and her children.

In black despair, Boyd remembered that during the war, in an idle moment, he had picked up a copy of Mrs. Eddy's *Science and Health with Key to the Scriptures* somewhere, and had tossed it into his duffel. He retrieved it from the attic and began to read. "For the first time," he says today, "something clicked inside me and I said to myself, 'This makes sense. This, I can believe about God.' " He consulted a practitioner who— much to Boyd's disappointment—wasted no sympathy on him. "He sent me home to read and pray," Boyd recalls, "and said that he and God would help me."

The way back was hard. In Christian Science, all drugs, medicines, tobacco, liquor—or any trait to which man can become a slave, such as jealousy, sexual obsession, envy—must be discarded in order that God's love may take hold of the mind. Carroll Boyd gave up liquor, tobacco (he was a heavy smoker), the habit of lying abed until noon, profane speech. He turned his thoughts to constructive goals: love for his family, who had not deserted him in his crisis; love of God, who, being perfect, had made man spiritually perfect too. Soon, out of the blue, he had a good job. He straightened up, began to think clearly. He started to attend the Christian Science Church. His daughter, about to be confirmed in another denomination, was asked to try the Science Sunday school for a year. Rebelliously, she did so. At the end of the year, she voluntarily stayed on.

Today, Carroll Boyd has a responsible job as traffic manager in a big long-haul trucking company. He handles the daily crises of that arduous business with unruffled calm.

In York, as everywhere, Scientists constantly run into little conflicts between Principle and community custom. They see no value in vaccinations, inoculations or physical examinations. But the Federal Government requires a vaccination certificate for re-entry after a trip abroad; military inductees undergo a battery of inoculations and are sent to sick call and hospitals. York Scientists follow these and other practices without argument, rather than create an issue. In childbirth, Scientists call a doctor to use, not his medicine, but his skills.

Funerals are held in mortuary chapels or private homes, usually with the first reader offering a few selections from the Bible and from Mrs. Eddy's writings. Scientists do not recognize death. Life to them is indestructible, therefore they "pass on" to a higher, unseen plane of existence.

Scientist women in York work in the Red Cross, but will not take blood from donors or handle medicines. Some York Scientists wear glasses, some consult dentists; a few, on rare occasions, may resort to drugs for acute pain. Here, they are on orthodox ground, for Mrs. Eddy recognized that perfection is difficult to achieve, and that most Scientists will fall short of it in some way, due to lack of understanding of Principle. No York Scientist drinks or smokes or uses harsh language.

In York, the reading room the church maintains is staffed twenty-six hours a week by church members. Traveling salesmen and other Scientists away from home stop by to read the weekly lesson. Local Scientists consult the complete files of church periodicals for help on specific problems. Non-Scientists who have heard Christian Science radio and TV programs often make first contact with the church through the reading room. At York, an average month attracts forty-seven readers, eighty-four purchasers of church papers and a half-dozen other visitors. Scientists know that, in any city, almost as many persons practice Christian Science outside the church as are members. At York, more than a hundred nonmembers habitually buy the *Quarterly,* in which are printed the weekly religious exercises. These "friends" usually attend the two free lectures a year sponsored by the York church. They also utilize the services of practitioners. Most of them are active members of other Christian denominations.

A Science publication known the world over is the *Christian Science Monitor,* a daily newspaper launched in 1908. Mrs. Eddy established it, not as a propaganda medium, but as an antidote to the yellow journalism then in vogue. The *Monitor* covers the news of the world, and carries only one Science article a day, on an inside page. The paper is unique in world journalism in that it is idealistic, searching for the good even in the most sordid details of war and crime. Its conservative journalism has had wide influence on the press at large. The *Monitor's* subscribers include 4,500 newspaper editors, chiefly non-Scientists, whose reprints of *Monitor* editorials and articles make the paper perhaps the most widely quoted daily in existence.

Scientists often are criticized for a lack of interest in human welfare. This they belied in World War II with a mighty contribution to world relief. Local committees were set in motion across the country, and by the war's end, they had spent $10,000,000 and distributed hundreds of tons of food and clothing in war areas and among refugees. At one period, of the 700 agencies in the United States contributing to war relief, the Christian Science Church ranked fourth in total effort. When the United States entered the war, Scientists had no ordained ministers to send as chaplains. They qualified more than 200 of their practitioners for duty under the title "wartime ministers"—a very high number, considering total church membership. There were also 26 Army and Navy chaplains. Scientists also set up 227 service centers in military camps and rest areas.

Christian Science was subjected to tough tests in the war. Hundreds of war-wound cures, many of them instantaneous, were claimed. In the past, some medical men have asserted that Christian Science claims of healing could not be validated because of improper diagnosis. During the war, military doctors themselves diagnosed many cases that Science says it subsequently cured.

In one case, a soldier's back was broken in two places, with the fractures clearly revealed by X-ray. The victim called a wartime minister to his bedside in an Army hospital. Next day, the doctor on his rounds discovered the patient absent from bed. Inquiry revealed the soldier in the mess hall having lunch. His back was said to be completely healed. It is also asserted that a soldier struck by lightning and pronounced dead by a doctor was revived by Science.

But healings were not the only demonstrations recorded. A Scientist, it is claimed, put a convoy of twenty-five-ton pieces of equipment across a six-ton bridge by application of Principle. An artillery battalion served by a Scientist chaplain fought from the Mediterranean through France and on to Austria without a combat death. In New Guinea, a patrol of thirty men was sent on a mission that appeared suicidal. A Scientist in the group began to speak aloud of his oneness with God. Others took up the words, repeating the phrases. The objective was taken; not a man was killed.

The theology of Christian Science has not changed since the passing of its founder. A bylaw permits no alterations in practice or interpretation without Mrs. Eddy's personal approval; neither can the bylaws be amended except by her. Therefore, Christian Science has reached its ultimate in organizational form and denominational outlook. All congregations are branches of the Mother Church in Boston, which strictly watches and quickly rebuffs any attempts to adulterate the faith as Mrs. Eddy left it a half century ago. Several serious attempts, including protracted lawsuits and revolts by individuals or congregations, have been made to break the rigidity of the *Manual* and the five-person rule of the Board of Directors. These revolts have all been firmly repudiated by a large majority of the membership.

Scientists proclaim that what Mary Baker Eddy left them was God-inspired, ultimate truth, and therefore needs no amendment. Within its framework, they hold, is contained everything required by mankind, not only for the personal needs of individuals, but also for the creation of a perfect world.

14

The Quakers

M ANY AMERICANS HAVE THE IDEA that the Quakers are a peculiar people who refuse to bear arms, shun politics and emphasize the utmost simplicity in speech, manner and dress. These prevailing notions about the Religious Society of Friends, the Quakers' formal name, are as obsolete as the Quaker bonnet.

There are still a few bonnets left, but the distinctive Quaker costume was discarded a half century ago. Far from avoiding politics, certain Quaker groups support a full-time staff of registered representatives in Washington, D. C. The Friends have had a President of the United States, Herbert Hoover, and a Vice-President, Richard M. Nixon. Although the Quaker tradition of pacifism is still strong, it is far from universal, and many Friends have served in the armed forces.

Another misconception is that all Quakers worship in silent assembly, without ministers, sermons, music or liturgy. The fact is that many Quaker meetings are more likely to resemble those of either the Congregationalists or the Southern Baptists. The use of the second-person-singular pronoun "thee" instead of "you," once a universal Quaker custom, is now rarely practiced outside the family. The ban on jewelry and on clothing with ornamental buttons has almost disappeared, along with other severe disciplines. The original mysticism of Quaker theology, which emphasized an "inner light," or direct communication with God, has lost much of its meaning for a majority of Friends.

There is no longer much that is quiet about the Quakers. Only a minority still practice clannish retirement from the world, or are content to be known as "peculiar." The American Friends Service Committee shared the Nobel Peace Prize in 1947 with the British Friends Service Council for world-wide labors in the cause of brotherhood. Today, the Friends have such a strong missionary program that Kenya colony, Africa, for example, has 28,000 Quakers. This is nearly 15 per cent of the world body of 194,022. In the United States, there are only a few more Quakers today (120,491) than during the American Revolution.

But while this country's Friends are few, their impact upon American life has been monumental. No religious group of any size in America has more obstinately championed peace and social justice, or had a more colorful history, than the Quakers.

The drama surrounding William Penn's Quaker colony in Pennsylvania has led many Americans to believe that the first Friends to reach the New World accompanied Penn, in 1682, up the Delaware River to the site of Philadelphia. Actually, a chain of Quaker communities stretched from New Hampshire to South Carolina ten years before Penn's arrival. Prior to 1680, four American Friends had been hanged, and scores had been tortured, martyrs to the cause of free religion.

Martyrdom was a fate that befell many Quakers almost from the time the movement was founded by George Fox. The son of a weaver in Leicestershire, England, he was born in 1624. He grew up buffeted by the religious turmoil that produced Oliver Cromwell, the Pilgrims and Puritans. Fox left home at nineteen and wandered for four years, seeking a Christianity that would put him into closer contact with God. His self-torment crystallized in the conclusion that all Christians were priests who might hold mystic communion directly with God, whom Fox defined as a spirit exemplifying love and truth. Fox concluded that ordained ministers and all liturgical forms of worship were unnecessary. Anyone who sat quietly, shutting the world from his thoughts, would be guided by the presence of God within—an inward spirit or "inner light." In Fox's view, everyone was sacred and equal.

What Fox preached was, in fact, a social revolution. Inherent in it was democracy in its highest form, with complete freedom for the individual to reach God in his own way. In 1654, Fox had only sixty followers. Five years later, he had thirty thousand. These early Quakers refused to doff their hats to a judge in court, or even to a king. They employed a "plain" language, addressing each other as "thee" because they thought "you" too formal to be used among equals, and held legal oaths to imply a double standard of truth. Because there was "that of God in every man," Fox's followers refused to bear arms against a fellow man, join the armed forces, or even sue a neighbor.

Fox was arrested 60 times and spent six years in prison. By 1662, there were 4,000 male Quakers in English jails, but the women and children carried on the crusade. Between 1650 and 1689, perhaps 15,000 Friends suffered because of their faith. Some 450 died. This is remarkable, particularly since the Friends were so loosely organized that they did not even have a name. The epithet "Quaker" was contemptuously assigned the group by a judge in Derby, England, before whom Fox was tried. Adjured by Fox to "quake with fear of the Lord," the magistrate derisively called Fox a "quaker," and the name became universal. Not until 1793 did the movement decide what to call itself. In this year, in an address to King George III, the Quakers referred to themselves for the first time as the Religious Society of Friends.

Fox taught that since men and women themselves are godly, and all are ministers, every act of their lives is performed in the presence of God. Thus no halfway allegiance is possible. A Quaker must be scrupulous in business and personal dealings, and truthful above reproach, and must live in love with everyone, even his enemies. He must also die, if required, for the faith. These beliefs caused many Friends to travel on self-financed missions, carrying their testimony throughout the world.

It was inevitable that some of these early emissaries should invade the Massachusetts Bay Colony of America, where the Congregationalists refused to tolerate any religious emphasis except that of Puritanism. Here was a challenge that the Friends could not ignore.

The issue was first taken up by two women. From the beginning, Friends have acknowledged women to be the equals of men, and probably half of the first-generation Quaker apostles were women. On July 11, 1656, Mary Fisher and Ann Austin reached Boston from London via Barbados.

The New England fathers knew about the Quakers and feared them. The colony was still torn by the controversy surrounding the banishment of Anne Hutchinson, and if there was anything likely to renew the storm, it was two more aggressive feminine dissenters. The Quaker women were jailed, and their books were burned. They were stripped naked by their jailers and examined for witch marks. During their five weeks' imprisonment, they were succored by a kindly Boston woman, Mary Dyer, who strongly supported their cause and was promptly banished, along with her husband, to Rhode Island. Mistresses Fisher and Austin were returned to Barbados by Massachusetts authorities. Two days after their departure, eight more Quakers arrived. They were detained for eleven weeks and sent packing, too, only to be replaced by Mary Dyer, who returned from Rhode Island with a companion, Ann Burden. Mistress Dyer was banished a second time.

The next arrivals in Boston found their way to the New World in one of the most fantastic maritime feats on record. In Yorkshire, England, Robert Fowler heard of the ignominy suffered by Friends in Boston and decided to make a witness of his own, testifying to his faith before the Puritans. With no knowledge of ship design, he built a little boat, descriptively named it the *Woodhouse* and sailed to London. There, he picked up six of the Quakers whom Boston had ostracized, plus five others. No experienced sailor would sign on with him, due to the crudeness of his vessel. So Fowler sailed the *Woodhouse* alone, without navigating instruments or any experience at sea, guided only by faith. He landed without incident on Long Island. From there, his passengers scattered to plant Quaker settlements from Cape Cod to the Carolinas.

The first Quaker in America to die for his cause, William Robinson, was one of the passengers on the *Woodhouse*. Together with another Quaker, Marmaduke Stephenson, he was hanged on Boston Common in 1659.

Ordered to die along with them was Mary Dyer. After having been twice banished from Boston, she had returned with Stephenson and Robinson. The rope was about her neck when she was reprieved. She was deported, but a year later, she turned up again. This time, she insisted on martyrdom. As she ascended the gallows, she was offered her freedom if she would promise to leave Massachusetts and never return. "Nay," she replied, "I cannot." A strong wind was blowing, and after the execution, a witness exclaimed "Look! She flies there like a flag." And so she did.

Her execution was the most dramatic martyrdom of a Quaker in America. When King Charles II heard of it, he directed a curt note to the Massachusetts authorities, commanding them to kill no more Quakers, but to dispatch them to England for trial. He sent as envoy to deliver this note one Samuel Shattuck—himself a

Boston-banned Quaker. In 1959, a statue to Mary Dyer was erected on the Statehouse lawn in Boston, overlooking the site of her death.

By the time Mary Dyer was put to death, there were flourishing Friends' meetings in Sandwich, Falmouth, Scituate and Salem, founded by others of the *Woodhouse* band. This cracked the Congregational monopoly, although legal penalties for preaching Quakerism, such as cropping of ears and floggings from town to town, continued until 1681.

George Fox visited America in 1672-73 and found firmly rooted groups of Friends all along the Atlantic seaboard. The largest concentrations were in Rhode Island, where half the population was Quaker, and in Maryland. New England Friends had formed a Yearly Meeting in 1661. This was a purely voluntary association of local meetings, without any denominational power. Maryland and Virginia Friends both organized Yearly Meetings while Fox was among them.

Fox was particularly pleased by the affluent freedom of New Jersey Quakers and carried this enthusiasm back to England, where plans were made for three Quaker-chartered colonies. The first of these "holy experiments" was established only two years after Fox's visit, when two English Friends, John Fenwick and Edward Byllynge, bought what was known as West Jersey from Lord Berkeley in 1674. The next year, Fenwick brought over a colony of Friends which settled at Salem, New Jersey. In 1679, East Jersey was bought by an English Quaker syndicate and became the second haven in America.

So when William Penn began his celebrated work in 1682, he discovered 1,400 Friends already settled in the Jerseys. Penn's great contribution was to prove to the world that a Quaker-inspired political organization could succeed. His treaty with the Indians, described by Voltaire as "the only treaty never sworn to and never broken," became a world model for the treatment of racial and religious minorities.

So honest was Quaker Pennsylvania that its paper money remained at par when every other colonial currency was falling in value. The colony's encouragement of free intellectual expression attracted such scientists as Benjamin Franklin and the botanist John Bartram. Its policy of a one-price marketing system, its freedom from Indian wars, its sobriety and thrift, and its general civil liberties (only one case of capital punishment was recorded prior to 1700) caused the settlement to become the wealthiest and most populous section of colonial America.

But a decline in Quaker power and influence began soon after. In the Carolinas and Jersey, Friends lost political control in 1702, after Queen Anne ascended the English throne and insisted on an oath of office. Friends could not comply. In 1756, they surrendered their rule of Pennsylvania and, within twenty years, were also unseated in Rhode Island, which had been dominated by thirty-six terms of Quaker governors. The Quaker decline was hastened during the Revolution. Because they could neither fight nor contribute funds for armament, they were persecuted by both sides. Mobs sacked their houses, two Quakers were hanged in Philadelphia, and twenty others were banished.

Gradually the Friends' movement waned from an aggressive social and political force and a fanatic missionary enterprise to an ingrown and almost dormant coterie. For 115 years—from 1698, when a Yearly Meeting in North Carolina joined those already in exis-. tence in New England, New York, Baltimore, Philadelphia-Jersey and Virginia—until 1813, when they added a Yearly Meeting in Ohio, the Friends recorded no new growth.

There were many causes for this torpor, in addition to the political situation. The Friends had no central authority to hold them together, no professional preachers to organize them, no creed, sacraments or declaration of faith about which to rally. Although they maintained many secondary schools, they supported no colleges at that time.

Their rejection of liturgical religion created a vacuum, which they filled with what they called the Discipline, setting up standards of conduct. These restrictions required utmost simplicity of dress and display, and a tenacious insistence on "plain" speech. They forbade dancing, drinking, gambling, fairs, wrestling, firearms, gossip and all worldly amusements, even art and music. Friends called non-Quakers "the world's people" to emphasize their own withdrawal. Any Friend who married out of meeting or violated the Discipline could be expelled from the society. The Quakers were proud to be known as a "peculiar people."

The original evangelistic fire sputtered out and was replaced by a quiet, sober, clannish reticence that became highly exaggerated over the years. One Friend in Rhode

Island, asked if he was ill, could not admit it. "I have a feeling that is akin to pain," he said. Thrift also was carried to great lengths. The story is told of a Philadelphian who, giving a young teacher a paper sack full of grapes, said, "Thee may keep the bag."

Business meetings were conducted—and most still are—without voting. Members, including women and children, rose and stated their cases in as few words as possible. When the clerk of the meeting, who sat in front but did not presume to be a chairman, felt that "the sense of the meeting" was unanimous, he wrote a "minute" in his book, and the matter was decided. If there was no agreement, the subject was simply laid over until a later date. One proposal was defeated in a Philadelphia meeting when an elder rose and said to the previous speaker, "I very largely agree with thee." This hedged answer was correctly interpreted as a vehement dissent.

So withdrawn were the Friends that they would not even call the days of the week or the months by name, since almost all are derived from pagan gods. They substituted the phrase "first day" for Sunday, for example, and October was designated simply "tenth month."

The Quakers' eccentricities lost them young people by the thousands. Often, in quiet meetings, not a word would be spoken for an hour, while an elder, seated facing the congregation, scowled upon any juvenile wiggling. When the elder decided the meeting had ended, he shook hands with the man seated next to him, thus dismissing the gathering. Anyone might preach, however, if he felt moved to do so, since Fox had taught that all Christians are priests. Often these volunteers were inspired to speak at length, in a singsong, monotonously musical delivery.

Young people who wished to marry were rigidly examined by a committee appointed by the monthly business meeting. If the fitness of the candidates was sustained, the bride and bridegroom were permitted to rise during worship, join hands and declare their marriage vows.

Frustrated in meeting, many Quakers "went outside" the movement to espouse the Friends' ideals. On the outside, they chipped away noisily at social evils. It is perhaps significant that two of the four great pioneer champions of women's rights were Quakers. The first was Lucretia Mott, founder of the feminist movement, outspoken abolitionist and prohibitionist, as well as the mother of six children.

Born on Nantucket into the celebrated Coffin family in 1793, Lucretia at 25 was recorded as a Quaker minister. On a trip to Virginia, she was appalled by slavery and began to preach against it in 1829. In 1842, she traveled 350 miles by carriage in Virginia, making antislavery speeches. She was carried into the feminist movement by indignation at being denied a delegate's seat at a World Antislavery Convention in London. With the Presbyterian, Elizabeth Cady Stanton, she called the Woman's Rights Convention, the first of its kind in the world, in 1848.

When Lucretia Mott finally retired at eighty-seven, an equally dedicated Quaker, Susan B. Anthony, continued the crusade. For much of her life, she plodded from state to state, seeking votes for women, their right to inherit money and property, and relaxed divorce laws for wives with drunken husbands. Teamed with Lucy Stone, a non-Quaker, Miss Anthony organized the International Congress of Women in 1888. By the time she retired, at seventy-nine, four states permitted women to vote in local elections, and a popular movement had begun that would result in passage of the Nineteenth Amendment.

Another voice heard across the land was that of John Greenleaf Whittier, the Quaker poet. His polemics against slavery did much to arouse New England sympathy for Negro slaves, and to rally Quakers into founding and operating the "Underground Railroad," which smuggled refugee slaves into Canada. Whittier's collected antislavery poems, *Voices of Freedom,* published in 1846, had a world impact. He gave up a career in politics and journalism to fight slavery.

And there was the late Rufus M. Jones, the "weightiest Quaker" of our own time. He was organizer and first chairman of the American Friends Service Committee. Jones also was instrumental in rousing Quakerism from its years of isolation. He wrote fifty-eight books inspiring Quakers to break out of what Elizabeth Gray Vining, another Friend and the postwar tutor of Japanese Crown Prince Akihito, has called the Quakers' "stagnation and decay."

Rufus Jones was born in 1863 at a time when the Friends were sundered by disputes that had divided them into two main factions and several isolated segments. The discord had begun to develop after the Revolution, when many Quakers moved westward. They were of two varieties: the quiet Friends of Philadelphia and its tradition, and the more boisterous children and converts of Quaker pioneers in Virginia and the Carolinas. The latter were forced from the South by the slavery issue. They moved chiefly to Ohio and Indiana. But they were not satisfied with the confinement of Philadelphia-style Quakerism. Many of them were accustomed to the revivalism of the Methodists, the fundamentalism of the Baptists and the strong leadership of paid preachers. They sang hymns, installed organs and choirs and hired pastors.

Even more divisive was the Westerners' insistence on a fundamentalist type of Christianity, rigidly based on the Bible. Many Easterners had become so liberal that they were theologically close to Unitarianism. In 1827-28, these conflicts split the Friends' movement down the middle. About half, some forty thousand, remained withdrawn, mostly liberal in theology and quiet in nonpastored meetings. The other half accepted denominationalism with prepared sermons and services little different in form from those of other evangelical-minded churches.

Rufus Jones, who was a teacher at Haverford College and editor of a Quaker paper, became the conciliator of Friendly differences. He proposed a new alignment of Friends, a Five Years Meeting to which most regional Yearly Meetings might subscribe. His argument was, in substance, that they were all united by the mysticism of

Quaker belief and by their common espousal of peace and humanitarianism. About two-thirds of all United States Quakers now belong to the Five Years Meetings. The other third belong either to the Friends General Conference or are independent.

But most Friends joined in supporting the American Friends Service Committee when it was set up in 1917. This committee, and two other later organizations, the Friends World Committee and the Friends Committee on National Legislation, have made the Quakers world-renowned. The Service Committee has fed refugees and tended the wounded in every armed conflict since World War I. The volume of this effort is formidable. After World War I, the Friends for a time fed more than one million German children every day.

Anywhere in the world that military action threatens to explode, from Indonesia to Cuba, the Friends act as the shock troops of mediation, conciliation and relief. One important aim of the Service Committee is to eliminate causes of international tension. Hence, it arranges conferences between diplomats, resettles refugees, combats illiteracy, sponsors foreign-exchange students and maintains an active observer staff at the United Nations.

In 1938, Rufus Jones demonstrated the Quaker approach to world problems when he undertook a mission to Nazi Germany. With two other Friends, he went directly to the Gestapo in Berlin to plead for fair treatment for Germany's Jews, and to work out a program by which many Jews were resettled abroad.

In 1943, some Quakers from all factions united to sponsor the Friends Committee on National Legislation, which is registered with Congress. The objective is to translate Christian ideals into political and social realities through legislation. The committee opposes capital punishment and military conscription. It works for disarmament and liberal immigration laws. Co-operating with other national groups, it mobilized some seventy-one thousand letters to Congress supporting a bill to insure civilian control of atomic energy.

The intense Quaker concern for peace persists, despite a significant decline in pacifist sentiment among younger members. There has never been solidarity on this "witness." In the Revolution, 400 Quakers were dismissed from the society for war activity, including the flag-maker Betsy Ross and General Nathanael Greene. In World War I, pacifism was the exception; there were an estimated 350 Quaker conscientious objectors, compared with 2,300 Friends in the armed forces. In World War II, there were 9,000 Quakers in uniform, although many were assigned to alternative service.

Quaker unity still faces obstacles. While the old differences among Quakers are healing, another schism is developing. An Association of Evangelical Friends, so far recruited entirely from individuals rather than from Yearly Meetings, now claims about one-sixth of all American Quakers, or about twenty thousand. Several independent Yearly Meetings, notably Ohio, Kansas and Oregon, have given strong support to the new movement, and perhaps half the members of the Five Years Meeting (the largest Quaker group) are openly sympathetic. The Association advocates fundamentalism, the emphasis being on primitive Christianity.

But of whatever stamp their theology, Friends today have emerged into the world again, with the conviction that their dispassionate, selfless concern for the great Christian ideals makes their world-wide humanitarianism uniquely effective. This witness they are now eager to spread throughout the world. They are encouraged by such incidents as one that occurred during the Mau Mau uprising in Kenya. The disturbance flared right up to the boundary of the Friends' missionary field, and there it stopped suddenly.

The Quakers appreciate particularly, for its many implications, the story of the Friend who was subpoenaed to testify in court. As he mounted the witness stand, the judge, knowing he was a Quaker, asked him, "Do you swear or affirm?"

"Neither," the Quaker answered. "I speak the truth."

"Very well," said the judge. "You may proceed."

Index

251